PRO TACTICS™ SERIES

PRO TACTICS™

WHITETAIL HUNTING

Expert Strategies and Techniques for a Successful Hunt

Bob Humphrey

LYONS PRESS

Guilford, Connecticut

An imprint of Globe Pequot Press

To the two most important women in my life:

To my wife, Jane, who has endured my frequent and often long absences during deer season and who seems to understand my need to seek solace, challenge, and success in the deer woods.

To my mother, who supported and encouraged my early interest in hunting and who saw to it that I never wanted for anything that I truly needed.

To buy books in quantity for corporate use or incentives, call **(800) 962–0973** or e-mail **premiums@GlobePequot.com**.

Copyright © 2011 Robert C. Humphrey

ALL RIGHTS RESERVED. No part of this book may be reproduced or transmitted in any form by any means, electronic or mechanical, including photocopying and recording, or by any information storage and retrieval system, except as may be expressly permitted in writing from the publisher. Requests for permission should be addressed to Globe Pequot Press, Attn: Rights and Permissions Department, P.O. Box 480, Guilford, CT 06437.

Lyons Press is an imprint of Globe Pequot Press.
Pro Tactics is a trademark of Morris Book Publishing, LLC.
Photos © Robert C. Humphrey unless otherwise credited
Project editor: Julie Marsh
Text designer: Peter Holm (Sterling Hill Productions) and Libby Kingsbury
Layout artist: Melissa Evarts

Library of Congress Cataloging-in-Publication Data

Humphrey, Bob.
  Pro tactics. Whitetail hunting : expert strategies and techniques for a successful hunt / Bob Humphrey.
      p. cm. — (Pro tactics series)
  Includes index.
  ISBN 978-1-59921-789-5
  1. White-tailed deer hunting. I. Title. II. Title: Whitetail hunting : expert strategies and techniques for a successful hunt.
  SK301.H846 2011
  799.2'7652—dc22

                                                                        2010020219

Printed in China

10 9 8 7 6 5 4 3 2 1

The author and Globe Pequot Press assume no liability for accidents happening to, or injuries sustained by, readers who engage in the activities described in this book.

CONTENTS

FOREWORD BY CHARLES ALSHEIMER

Where were you when you saw your first white-tailed deer? What lasting impression did it leave?

I had my first encounter when I was six years old. On the eve of deer season, my dad and I were driving down a dirt road on our New York potato farm. From the driver's side a huge buck jumped the roadside ditch, hit the road in one bound, and ran across a plowed field and out of sight. The scene lasted little more than ten seconds, but the vision of the buck's massive rack and muscular body is forever imprinted on my mind. In many ways that sight birthed my career in the outdoor field.

Millions of outdoorsmen have similar stories. It's safe to say no other animal has such a loyal following as the white-tailed deer. It's Earth's most majestic animal.

When the first settlers arrived in North America, they found a paradise teeming with wildlife. Even then, the white-tailed deer was the dominant big-game species. Centuries before European settlers arrived, Indians relied heavily on the whitetail for food, clothing, and tools.

It's not known exactly how many whitetails inhabited North America when the Pilgrims landed at Plymouth Rock. Some estimate that the whitetail population was as high as 40 million. Others say there were fewer than 20 million, about 10 million fewer than today's estimated population.

At any rate, deer numbers steadily plummeted as the continent was settled. The American spirit for adventure pushed settlers westward; they cleared land for farming and industry and shot deer indiscriminately for food and leather. With year-round hunting, no bag limits, and high demand for leather and venison in cities and logging camps, market hunting boomed across the whitetail's range. By the late 1800s their numbers had crashed to fewer than 500,000.

Around 1900 a plea went out to America's sportsmen to regulate deer-hunting seasons. Unfortunately, the damage was already done, and it took decades for healthy herds to rebuild. In the 1930s, '40s, and '50s deer seasons began to open regularly throughout the East and Midwest.

Still, not until the late 1970s did we get our first true glimpse of the white-tail's incredible potential, both as a game animal and as the driving force in the hunting industry. When it comes to hunting, the whitetail has no peers. It is the most sought-after and studied animal on Earth. Commercially, it is the reason there is a thriving industry surrounding hunting. Without the whitetail there would be no firearms, archery, hunting apparel, or hunting accessory industry. Of the roughly $35 billion spent on hunting in America today, over $25 billion is generated by white-tailed deer. The whitetail is not just the straw that stirs the hunting drink but the drink itself.

The whitetail's popularity causes millions of deer hunters to head for the woods each fall. And in nearly every case, today's deer hunters strive to be more knowledgeable about both their quarry and methods of pursuit. In order to reach their goals, hunters look to whitetail experts to enable them to become better hunters. One such expert is Bob Humphrey of Pownal, Maine.

I knew of Bob Humphrey's whitetail expertise through his many magazine articles well before I ever shook his hand for the first time. When our paths finally crossed at a writers' conference, I quickly realized he was unique to the deer-hunting industry. What sets him apart from many other communicators is that he is both an accomplished whitetail hunter and a professional wildlife biologist. He has the unique ability to speak both the hunter's and the biologist's languages and be able to blend them into a package all can understand. This gift has allowed him to tell both the hunter's and the whitetail's stories, as few in America can.

In the pages that follow, you undoubtedly will learn many new and wonderful things about the whitetail. From chapter 1, which deals with natural history, biology, and behavior, to the last chapter, which discusses how to introduce youngsters to the world of hunting, you'll find loads of insightful information.

Between these covers Bob Humphrey will show you the whitetail's beauty, grace, intelligence, wariness, and, yes, those magnificent antlers that stir the hunter's imagination. When you are finished with this book, you'll have a better understanding of why the white-tailed deer is so loved by millions of America's outdoorsmen.

One thing is certain: *Pro Tactics*: *Whitetail Hunting* will surely add to your whitetail addiction. It's a book all will enjoy and learn from, whether you are a teenager just starting out or a deer hunter with over half a century under his belt. You are in for a real treat—enjoy the journey.

Charlie Alsheimer
Northern Field Editor
Deer & Deer Hunting magazine

ACKNOWLEDGMENTS

There are so many who, knowingly or otherwise, contributed to this book. Virtually everyone I crossed paths with in the deer woods, hunting camps, outdoor shows, and seminars all played some part in my deer-hunting experiences, which are woven into the fabric of these pages.

The list begins with the Poverty Mountain Boys, with whom I shared my first deer-hunting adventures: Jon Andrews, Mark Luthman, Chris Ricardi, and Jim Farquhar. We were all wide-eyed undergraduate wildlife biology students who spent every possible moment we could in the local woodlots chasing pheasants, rabbits, ducks, and, of course, deer. We eventually expanded our hunting horizons to the far reaches of the continent, and we still try to share a hunt together now and then.

I owe a great deal of credit for my first deer to Gary Foster, now a biologist with the West Virginia Division of Natural Resources. Gary is a friend and former college mate of Mark's who was kind enough to host us on our first road trip, to the mountains of West Virginia. Seeing so many deer, I was like a kid in a candy shop, and tagging that first buck gave me the confidence I needed to go back home and do it again a few weeks later.

While there are many who have been helpful, a few individuals were instrumental in advancing my career as an outdoor writer: Steve Carpenteri at Game & Fish publications, who had enough faith in me to give me some of my first important writing assignments; Ken Piper, now editor of *Buckmasters*, who gave me plenty of feature assignments and my first magazine column in *New England Outdoor Times* and has since become a good friend; Stu Bristol, who became a mentor to me in my early years as a writer; and Jay Strangis, former editor of *Petersen's Bowhunting*, who gave me some of my first breaks in the big leagues.

Then there are those folks who contributed more directly to the content of this book:

Dave Dolbee (*Petersen's Bowhunting*), who has been a reliable and ongoing source for technical archery information and is a pleasure to share deer camp with;

Bob Foulkrod, considered one of the best in the business, for his thoughts on recovering wounded game;

Dick "the Deer Tracker" Bernier, who shared his insights from more than thirty years of tracking big-woods bucks;

Brad Harris and Mark Drury, for their thoughts on deer calling;

Judd Cooney, with whom I had the pleasure of sharing a deer camp in Alabama, for advice on rattling;

Pat McHugh (MPIOutdoors) for information on packs;

Bill Winke, for his stunning photography;

Ben Maki (Mossy Oak) for advice and information on clothing;

My old buddy Ron Bice (Wildlife Research Center) for support and information on scents and lures;

Mike Jordan (ATSKO) for information on deer vision and scent suppression;

Mike Disario and Glenn Chappelear (Outdoor Expeditions International) for tips on booking a hunt and for sending me around the country to hunt and photograph whitetails;

Craig and Neal Dougherty (North Country Whitetails);

And Charlie Alsheimer for information on building food plots.

Becoming a successful deer hunter is a rite of passage. For me the journey began in the hills of Western Massachusetts. Actually, it was one hill in particular, Poverty Mountain, where I took those first steps on my deer-hunting odyssey.

It was a warm Indian summer afternoon, and we were pheasant hunting along the fallow edges of a cornfield when I noticed heart-shaped impressions in the soft, dark soil. I'd seen them before and never really paid them much mind. But for some reason that day was different.

Suddenly, my interest was piqued. I noticed that the deer seemed to be entering the field at one location and leaving at another. "It shouldn't be too difficult to shoot one," I thought. "All I have to do is set up on one of those trails at the right time and wait them out." Boy, was I wrong.

Things were very different back then for deer hunters. It was a time when bragging rights went to anyone who saw a deer. Being drawn for a doe tag was akin to winning the lottery, and the breadth of deer-hunting information upon which to draw was minuscule compared to today.

All the same, my cronies and I gave it our best effort. Day after day we'd arrive before daylight and sit on the hills above the field, waiting for deer to leave the corn. In the afternoon we'd set up low, anticipating hungry deer marching down the hillsides to feed. In between, we wore ourselves ragged trekking the hills.

It was on one such late-morning jaunt that I first saw them. My eyes were downcast, studying tracks, when I heard a commotion ahead. I looked up in time to see several white flags dancing away through the timber. I was awestruck.

Racing to the spot where I'd last seen the deer, I found where their hooves had overturned leaves and kicked up dirt. I was surprised at how easy those tracks were to follow on the dry leaves, but I was even more surprised to look up and see the deer that made them, barely 100 yards away. Again they bolted, and again I followed. Because I was carrying a bow, I didn't really expect to get close enough for a shot, but for the first time in my life, I really felt that I was hunting deer.

Little did I know that those first steps would eventually lead me on a quest from the northern forests of Maine and the suburbs and woodlots of mid-Atlantic states, down the Appalachians, through the bottomland swamps of the Southeast and Deep South to the harsh and forbidding brush country of West Texas, up through the agricultural heartland of the Midwestern breadbasket, along the Rockies and into the dense forests of Canada.

What began as mild curiosity soon turned to a passion, bordering on obsession. My quest to succeed was fueled by an

■ Learning more about the game you pursue will make for a more successful and enjoyable hunting experience.

urge to learn as much about these fascinating creatures as I could. And I soon discovered that the more I learned, the more successful I became.

Success

That is what this book is about: being successful at hunting whitetails. There are many definitions of success. For some, success means bagging a trophy buck—and there is probably a similarly large number of definitions for the word *trophy*. For others it means taking a particular deer, perhaps a sagacious old buck they've been chasing for several seasons. Still others might define success as meat on the

pole or that all-important first deer. And finally, there are those who define success less by what they bring home in the back of their truck and more by what they bring home in their hearts and minds.

This book is designed for all deer hunters, regardless of how you define success—whether you're hunting outside your back door or planning the trip of a lifetime. No doubt the title will conjure up all sorts of expectations for deer hunters from each of the above categories. Hopefully, most will be met and perhaps some exceeded.

Perhaps you'll find something that will help you bag that buck of a lifetime, tie your tag on your first buck, or merely

■ **From tiny acorns mighty oaks grow. These little fawns may one day grow to stir the heart of some hunter.**

gain a much greater appreciation for the animal you pursue.

For whitetails truly are magnificent animals.

Consider that they've been around for at least four million years. They have adapted to survive in habitats as harsh and contrasting as the northern forests of Canada and the deserts of Mexico and just about everywhere in between. Before two-legged predators came along, whitetails not only survived ecological disasters, such as fires and floods, but learned how to exploit them and even withstood ice ages.

Man entered the picture only very recently, and for 10,000 years, whitetails served as a major source of food and worship. Then the Europeans found a

foothold in North America, and in the blink of a geologic eye, the continent was transformed. By the late eighteenth century, North America was fully colonized, and over the next 100 years, whitetails were commercially exploited to the brink of extinction. It seemed the whitetail had met its match at last.

Enter the modern conservation movement. Prompted by cries from, of all people, hunters, states began implementing restrictions, such as bag limits and closed seasons. Whitetails quickly rebounded from perhaps as few as 100,000 individuals to more than 30 million today. And they have learned not only to survive but to thrive in and around the trappings of man. They are the most popular and most sought-after game animal on the continent, perhaps in the world.

As you read through the pages ahead, think about what success means to you, and remember that success is fleeting. For as soon as you achieve one success, you'll begin setting higher goals and placing more obstacles in front of yourself. And one day, perhaps, you'll realize that it is the journey, not the end, that is most important.

Remember, too, that this book is designed primarily to help you *begin* your journey in the right direction. There is no substitute for experience. Every hunt, whether it ends successfully or not, teaches a lesson that can be used toward future success. Read on, learn, and enjoy.

CHAPTER ONE

Natural History, Biology, and Behavior

What a marvelous creature is the white-tailed deer. Mysterious, cunning, and beautiful, it holds the fascination of more hunters than any other creature, and it would likely take a team of biologists, psychologists, and anthropologists to even begin to understand why.

I too have been enchanted by the whitetail's siren song, and one of the most important lessons I've learned in roughly a quarter century of deer hunting is that in order to be consistently successful you need to be a student of the animal you pursue. Knowing such techniques as how to use certain types of calls or scents is useful, but if you don't know why you're using them, or when they're most effective, their utility is limited.

There are myriad volumes of information from which you can learn how to be a more successful hunter, and this is but one more. The best teacher, though, is the animal itself, and there is no substitute for experience. That experience becomes all the more valuable when you can understand and interpret what you observe.

So let's begin with a basic introduction to the white-tailed deer. As you learn more and more about the animal and its habits, you can begin concentrating on the finer points. This knowledge will also make for a safer and more enjoyable hunt. Watching a randy buck chase a doe hither and yon through the woodlot is thrilling, but understanding why he's chasing will give you a much greater appreciation for what you're about to become a part of as you move in to challenge him.

Biologically Speaking

Taxonomically, the whitetail is a member of the order *Artiodactyla*—even-toed ungulates, or animals that walk on paired hooves. And deer do indeed walk on four pairs of hooved digits, which make those heart-shaped impressions that stir the blood of any hunter. When they are fleeing danger, their long, powerful legs can propel them up to nearly 40 miles per hour. They can clear a 7-foot vertical obstacle from a standing start and cover more than 30 feet of distance in a single bound.

This order includes pigs, deer, and bovines. The latter two groups are termed ruminant artiodactyls because of the way and their lifetime. Here, they regurgitate a lump of food (called a bolus or cud) from the reticulum so it can be rechewed. This provides for more effective mechanical breakdown of the roughage deer consume.

Food Habits

Deer are generally classified as herbivores, plant eaters. It would take an entire chapter to cover adequately the range of foods deer find palatable, for they are fairly non-specific and their diet varies considerably by geographic location. It also varies by season, as food availability and nutritional requirements change. In the spring and summer, deer are predominantly grazers, feeding on herbaceous vegetation, such as grasses and forbs, particularly those high in protein. Does need the added protein to bear and rear fawns, and bucks need it for body and antler growth. In the fall, as herbaceous vegetation becomes scarce and deer must lay on fat for the coming winter, they switch to browse and high-calorie mast.

Whitetails are the most numerous and widespread North American member of the *Cervidae* family, which also includes mule deer, elk, and caribou. Their scientific name, *Odocoileus virginianus*—the Virginia white-tailed deer—refers to their dentition and the origin of some of their earliest fossil remains.

The whitetail's range extends from Canada south through the United States and into Mexico and Central America.

■ The white-tailed deer is the most popular big game animal in North America, and quite possibly the world.

they digest food. Ruminants have a four-chambered stomach; they actively feed for short periods of time, storing as much food as they can in the first chamber, the reticulum. They then retire to bed, where they spend a considerable portion of their day

■ White-tailed deer are ruminants. After feeding, they retire to secluded bedding areas, where they spend a considerable portion of their day, and their lifetime, digesting their food.

Within that range scientists have further classified them into roughly thirty subspecies. They vary in a number of ways but generally tend to get smaller as you move from north to south.

Home on the Range

An oft-repeated generalization is that a deer will live its entire life within a square-mile area. This is true, to some extent, particularly for does. For every rule, however, there is an exception. The size of an individual deer's home range can vary considerably, depending on the quality and quantity of available habitat; the better the habitat, the smaller the range. Mature

bucks, meanwhile, will spend most of the year in a small core area but may travel as far as 5 or 10 miles in search of does during the rut.

A young deer spends roughly the first year of its life in its mother's home range. At six months of age, some deer are driven off by mature bucks courting does. The following spring, as she nears birthing,

■ In the northern part of their range, whitetails make annual migrations to traditional wintering areas or deer yards.

a mature doe may also drive off her off-spring from the previous year.

The young does will often set up a new home range around the perimeter of their mother's. Biologists refer to this as the clover-leaf effect. During the rut, young bucks are driven out into unfamiliar territory. This, along with their relative lack of experience, is the reason they are so vulnerable to hunters. Those that survive their first fall may set up a new range far from where they were born; this mechanism helps prevent inbreeding.

When we think of migration in the deer family, we usually envision vast herds of caribou trekking hundreds of miles across the tundra or elk and mule deer moving down out of the mountains, ahead of the deepening snow. Some whitetails also move several miles on a seasonal basis. Small-scale migrations take place as a result of localized food availability. In the West, as whitetails continue to expand their range into higher elevations, they make seasonal, altitudinal migrations down from the high country in the late fall.

The most dramatic examples, however, occur in the northern range of the whitetail, where they make annual migrations to traditional wintering areas or yards. In forested regions these are usually low-lying areas dominated by coniferous forest, which help mitigate the cold and snow. However, in the plains and prairies, the wintering areas may be merely south-facing slopes.

Physical Characteristics

Deer are sexually dimorphic, meaning males (bucks) and females (does) have different physical characteristics. The most obvious difference is that females, for the most part, lack antlers. Occasionally, a female will sport antlers, usually the result of abnormally high testosterone levels. As previously mentioned, weights vary according to subspecies, but in more northern populations an average

■ In summer deer wear a russet coat of very thin hair to help them dissipate heat.

■ Occasionally, deer will sport a coat of mottled white and brown. A deer with this genetic trait is referred to as a piebald.

■ Nature's art, antlers are among the fastest-growing tissues in the animal kingdom. Each year a buck sheds his antlers and grows an entirely new set.

adult female will have a dressed weight of approximately 100 pounds, while an average adult male will weigh about 150 pounds. The whitetail is actually shorter than most people realize; adults stand about 36 inches tall at the shoulder.

The Five Senses

Whitetails have five senses that they use to find food, communicate, and avoid danger, though most hunters would swear they have a sixth sense for the latter.

Vision

A deer is prey, not a predator. Its eyes are located on the sides of its head rather than in the front, so it has a much broader field of view—roughly 310 degrees. It also has two blind spots. One is just in front of its nose, the other is a 50-degree arc, directly behind it.

A deer's three-dimensional binocular vision is more limited than our own, so it has poorer depth perception, except directly in front of it. However, it focuses on a banded area rather than a specific point, which gives it a much wider field of view but with less detailed focus.

A deer's eyeballs differ from ours in other ways, too. Its pupil opening is three times the size of a human's. According to Dr. Karl Miller of the University of Georgia, that means nine times the light-gathering ability. Furthermore, the back of a deer's eye has a light-reflecting organ called the tapetum, which effectively doubles light-gathering ability, bringing it up to 18 times that of a human.

Eyes of all animals have rods and cones; rods detect light, cones color. Deer have far more rods than we do, further enhancing their ability to see in darker conditions.

However, they have fewer cones, which reduces their color perception. According to Miller, deer perceive color much as a human with color blindness would. They see blues, greens, and yellows very well, but orange and red appear only as different shades of gray. That means they do not see blaze orange.

Some laundry detergents contain fabric brighteners. Essentially, they change the wavelength of colors, bringing them out of the ultraviolet range into the blue range we humans can see. This is also the range where deer have the highest color-detection ability. Some products, often

We really don't know how much better a deer's sense of smell is than ours, though varying sources have plugged it at between 20 and 10,000 times greater. Clearly, it is the single most important obstacle for the deer hunter to overcome. Deer have several sets of glands that secrete pheromones, which give off the scent used to communicate with one another (something we'll look at more closely in chapter 11).

Hearing

Deer use their sense of hearing for predator detection and communication. Their large ears are well designed to capture sound and funnel it into the inner ear cavity. Anyone who's ever watched an alert deer has seen how it constantly shifts the position of its ears as it scans for sounds.

Taste and Feel

Less is known about how deer use the senses of taste and feel. Clearly, they use taste to differentiate palatable foods from nonpalatable ones. Touch is probably the deer's least important sense. They have long bristles on their muzzles and eyelashes, which they use to avoid obstacles as they move through the forest.

Behavior

Communication

Deer communicate with one another in a variety of ways, including physical gestures and the aforementioned vocalizations and scent. We'll address the latter two in more

■ Vision, hearing, and scent are the whitetail's three major senses used for detecting and avoiding predators.

called UV-killers, are now available to counteract the effect of fabric brighteners. The name is actually a bit of a misnomer because deer don't see into the UV range. But these products do work because they reduce the reflectivity of colors in the blue and purple range.

Smell

The deer's sense of smell is one of its most important. It uses this sense to detect danger, to locate food, and to communicate.

■ Deer communicate in a variety of ways, including physical gestures, vocalizations, and scent.

detail in later chapters. Probably the gesture most familiar to hunters is the erect white tail from which this species gets its common name. It represents a danger signal, though the exact purpose is still not completely understood. It may be merely an alert to other deer, a means for younger deer to follow their mother in thick cover, a means to confuse predators, or some combination of all these. The foot stomp is another, less dramatic gesture that signals danger or that something is not quite right.

Bucks use several gestures to signal aggression. Because it's dangerous, fighting is usually a last resort, and bucks will do several things to signal their agitation before resorting to combat. Ears laid back and a stiff-legged gait are signs of aggression. Sometimes an agitated buck will also erect the hairs on its back, a gesture called a pyloric erection. Bucks will also sometimes paw the ground like an angry bull to intimidate a rival.

When scent-checking a doe during the rut, a buck may stretch out his neck and curl his lip back in a behavior known as flehmen. This behavior has been recorded in other cervids and even some of the big cats and is believed to be a means of delivering scent to a scent-detecting organ on the roof of the mouth known as the vomeronasal organ.

Reproduction: The Rut

The rut is probably the most studied yet most misunderstood aspect of whitetail biology. Rutting behavior consists of several phases that extend over a three- to four-month period. It begins in the early fall, when diminishing daylight detected by the pineal gland triggers an increase in testosterone in bucks. This in turn causes a shunting of blood supply to the antlers. The first visible effect is that velvet dies, dries, and peels off the antlers.

This increase in testosterone also triggers an increase in aggressive behavior in bucks. Low-level aggressive encounters begin as bucks start sorting out the local dominance hierarchy (pecking order). These encounters are often very casual and may consist of delicate intermeshing (tickling) of antlers and some pushing. Between bouts bucks may actually groom each other, licking the face and ears of their rival, or they may feed peacefully side by side. These first sparring matches are often among bucks of similar age or social stature, and older bucks may react with indifference to challenges from younger, smaller bucks.

That won't be the case for long, however. As levels of testosterone and aggression continue to increase, sparring soon gives way to more purposeful combat. More dominant bucks become increasingly less tolerant of their subordinates and will

■ In early fall, sparring matches are often very casual and may consist of delicate intermeshing (tickling) of antlers and some pushing. Between bouts bucks may actually groom each other, licking the face and ears of their rival, or they may feed peacefully side by side.

try to drive them out of their home range. Fights among evenly matched dominant bucks are uncommon, but when they occur, they are intense and may result in one or both bucks being severely injured or killed.

While bucks are sorting out order among themselves, they are also beginning the process of locating a mate. The onset of what most hunters consider the true rut begins with rubbing and scraping. Deer actually do both throughout the year, but frequency and intensity increase dramatically approaching the breeding season.

Scrape Making

A buck begins scrape making by pawing the earth with its hooves, simultaneously depositing scent from its interdigital glands. Once a scrape is made, the buck will often urinate in it. Sometimes he will rub urinate—meshing the tarsal glands on the inside of his hocks together while urinating on them so that both urine and glandular scents are deposited on the scrape. This is presumed to be a means for the dominant buck to signal his status to other bucks and perhaps his readiness to breed to does.

All active scrapes have an overhanging branch, roughly five to six feet above. Deer that visit the scrape will often rub their foreheads and preorbital glands on this branch, which is sometimes referred to as a licking branch. This is believed to be another way that deer use scent to communicate with one another.

Estrus

The ever-dwindling daylight next triggers an increase in estrogen in does. Eventually, they will begin coming into estrus, or heat. This is fairly synchronous on the local level, which means most does will come into estrus at roughly the same time. However, the level of synchronicity can vary considerably and may be influenced by age and sex ratios, with does in less balanced populations being less synchronous.

The estrous cycle lasts approximately twenty-eight days. A few does will come into heat nearly a month before the rest, but most will experience their first estrous cycle during the peak of rut. Does that are not bred during their first estrous cycle will come into heat again twenty-eight days later. Some yearlings and older or sick does may come into their first estrus during this later, second rut as well.

The Stand is a term for the period when a doe is in estrus and willing to copulate with a buck. This generally lasts about twenty-four hours, and during this period, a tending buck will not leave his doe. It can be a trying time for the doe, as the buck continually chases her, nosing her rump, and sometimes even jabbing her with his antlers. As a result, does can become extremely skittish and secretive at this time.

Shortly after mating, the buck leaves the doe in search of another mate. In populations with a well-balanced sex and age ratio, most of the breeding is done by mature, dominant bucks. Younger bucks are capable of breeding and may do more in poorly balanced populations. This sometimes results in a more protracted, less intense rut.

Circadian Rhythms

Deer are considered crepuscular, meaning they are most active at twilight. But they are quite flexible in their daily activity patterns, and times of peak activity can vary in response to environmental variables, human activities, or other inexplicable influences. For example, deer on Anticosti Island, which lacks predators, are active throughout the day. Conversely, deer in most heavily hunted areas can become largely nocturnal.

Weather, temperature, and even barometric pressure can influence levels of deer activity. Heavy wind, rain, or snow can reduce or extinguish deer movement, though they may actually move more under the heavy overcast skies during a light rain. In the fall deer change their coat from a light, reddish pelage of thin hair to a dense, brownish gray coat made up of hollow hairs, which help them retain body heat. This is an asset when it's cold but a liability when it's warm. And studies of northern deer have shown that once they grow their heavy winter coat, daytime movement nearly ceases when temperatures rise much above 45 degrees Fahrenheit.

The barometer is probably the deer hunter's most underutilized tool. Like all animals, deer can sense the falling pressure of an approaching storm and will often be

■ **Weather, temperature, and even barometric pressure all influence deer activity levels.**

out feeding in earnest ahead of the low. Activity may be lower during low-pressure periods and increase when the pressure begins going back up.

Lunar Cycles

How, or even if, the moon influences deer behavior is one of deer hunting's greatest unsolved mysteries. Many, from pure recreationists to trained scientists, have tried to prove or disprove the concept. Recent years have seen a growing number of theories related to moon phase and position.

One of the most widely accepted beliefs is that during the full moon, deer move more at night and less during the day. The explanation often given is that deer can feed all night under moonlight, where they feel more comfortable, and thus won't need to move much during the day. That seems both reasonable and logical. And both scientific and anecdotal evidence appears to support it.

For decades both the scientific and hunting communities concurred that the rut occurred at roughly the same time each year—though that time varied substantially from one geographic location to another. Then about fifteen years ago, a couple of guys set the whitetail hunting world on its ear when they began promoting a contradicting theory. Charles J. Alsheimer and Wayne Laroche contended that not only did timing of the rut vary considerably from year to year, but the timing was quite predictable and was based on moon phase.

Their investigations have been detailed and extensive, are based on scientific experiments conducted on other species, and make a lot of sense. They show a strong correlation between the whitetail breeding cycle and autumn moon phases. However, their experiments and results don't quite meet rigid scientific standards; in fact, there's a large body of scientific evidence to the contrary. Still, the theory remains popular.

Yet another popular theory is outdoor writer Jeff Murray's moon-position theory. Murray proposes that because the moon's gravitational pull is stronger when the moon is directly overhead, deer will be more active during these times. He even invented a Moon Wheel that allows you to determine when these peak times will occur. Though several scientific studies have been conducted, to date there is no formal research that supports the theory. Regardless, it too remains immensely popular.

In the final analysis we're left with more questions than answers. For many hunters, the hard, factual evidence provides a less satisfying conclusion. On the other hand, folklore based on generations of anecdotal evidence strongly supports some consistent trends about how the moon affects deer movement and behavior. Perhaps the best advice I can offer was given to me as a young wildlife biology student by one of my professors. He said when what you observe in nature differs from the textbooks, nature is right.

By now you're probably wondering how all this information can make you a more successful hunter. For starters, you know a little bit more about a deer's feeding habits—that it feeds actively for short periods of time, then rests for long periods while it digests. This alone could be hugely beneficial in speculating where a deer might be and what it might be doing during a particular time of day.

You also know how a deer uses its senses to avoid danger and to communicate so you can take steps to overcome its strengths and take advantage of its weaknesses. In the chapters ahead you'll learn more on how to apply this information, but for now let's move on with a look at some of the equipment you'll need.

CHAPTER TWO

Guns and Ammo

hat's the best choice for a deer gun? Step into any deer camp in North America and ask that question, and you'll get at least as many different answers as there are hunters in camp. The same could probably be said for loads. In some respects that's a good thing because, while picking the right gun is difficult, picking the wrong one is even more difficult.

What works for one hunter may not for another; and different circumstances, conditions, hunting styles, or regulations sometimes require different tools. Rather than trying to tell you what's best, and risk alienating half the readers (at least), I'll give you some options and let you choose what best fits your individual needs and conditions. Above all else, the most

■ While the mechanisms are largely the same, modern deer rifles are now available with a variety of features, such as synthetic stocks and stainless steel barrels, which make them more weather resistant and more accurate.

important thing is picking a gun you are comfortable with.

In terms of firearms type, you have four basic choices: rifle, shotgun, muzzleloader, or handgun. Which you choose may depend on several factors, including personal preference and regulatory restrictions. Having at least one of each will give you greater versatility and could extend your hunting time considerably.

Rifles

As they are the most popular and widely used, let's start with rifles, medium- to long-range weapons designed to fire a single projectile. Rifles are named for the lands and grooves—rifling—inside the barrel. This causes the bullet to spin as it passes through, which results in better aerodynamics—straighter flight. Within this broad category are lots of choices.

Action

Which action you choose is largely a matter of personal preference, though each type has its advantages and disadvantages. The simplest is the single-shot, break action. It's easy to use, easy to clean, and there aren't many moving parts to break or malfunction. The simple, efficient design is also easier and cheaper to build, making this action relatively inexpensive. Overall, it's a great choice for the new or young hunter.

Interestingly, you can find break actions at both ends of the price range. On the economical end are those designed

■ Bolt actions are probably the most popular style among deer hunters. They offer a solid-locking breech for improved accuracy, with a magazine feed for successive shots.

for beginners or budget-conscious hunters who prefer single-shot simplicity. They typically have a dull blue finish and plain hardwood (birch) stocks. Most well known among this group are those made by H&R and New England Firearms. The solid-locking breech, however, has the potential to be the most accurate action, which is why some manufacturers pair it with a precision quality barrel. A prime example is Thompson/Center's Contender and Encore lines.

The major disadvantage is that you sacrifice a quick follow-up shot. However, if you practice with your firearm and take only quality shots, you shouldn't need one. Break-action doubles are far more popular in Europe and Africa; you rarely see one in the North American deer woods.

Next up the ladder, and probably the most popular, is the bolt action. This style also offers a solid-locking breech for improved accuracy, typically with a magazine feed for successive shots. There are a few more moving parts, but bolt actions tend to be reliable. Both this and the break action are better suited, but certainly not limited, to the stationary hunter.

The primary advantage of repeaters—slide-actions, lever-actions, or semi-autos—is a very quick follow-up shot. This can be particularly advantageous to the mobile hunter who may be hunting in thick cover or may be shooting at moving game. With more moving parts there is a slightly higher chance for jams and mechanical failure, but most modern guns are so well made that these are fairly

rare occurrences, provided you keep your firearm well maintained.

Unlike the other repeaters, lever-actions and some slide-action rifles have tubular magazines. This limits your choice of ammunition to calibers made with round-nosed bullets because the bullets are held in a tip-to-primer configuration.

Caliber

One of the most frequently and hotly debated topics in deer camps all across America every fall is what is the best caliber for deer hunting. The short answer is: it depends. In more open country, where longer shots are possible, you might prefer a flatter-shooting cartridge. In dense cover, or when hunting larger deer of the north country, you may opt for a heavier

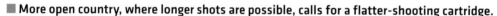
■ More open country, where longer shots are possible, calls for a flatter-shooting cartridge.

bullet. Stepping up to a magnum caliber gives you a broader range of application. Conversely, a younger or slighter hunter may prefer the reduced recoil offered by a lighter load.

The acceptable range of deer calibers runs the gamut, roughly from .243 to .45-70. Smaller, lighter calibers like the .243, 6mm, and .25-06 are flat-shooting but lower on the energy scale. They're best suited to stand hunting and shooting smaller deer in open country, where the hunter has time to take careful aim. The lighter recoil also makes them a better option for young or small-framed hunters.

In the middle of the recommended range for deer cartridges are some of the more popular choices like the .270, 7mm, .308, and .30-06. The .270 offers bullet weights from 130 to 150 grains, while the .308 ranges from roughly 150 to 180 grains. Versatility may be an important consideration for someone who only owns one deer rifle. The .30-06 is the versatility champion, offering a bullet range from 125 to 200 grains. The .308 is also a popular choice, as it offers similar ballistics to the .30-06 but may lack some of the top-end versatility for larger game. The .270 offers similar ballistics, toward the lighter end.

One way to increase velocity without sacrificing bullet weight or energy is to step up to a magnum caliber, such as the .300 Winchester Mag, or 7mm Remington Mag. A more recent development has been the short magnums: .270, 7mm, and .300 WSM (Winchester Short Magnum),

TAKING YOUR SHOT

National hunter-safety programs strongly discourage shooting at running deer. Ultimately, it is up to the individual hunter's discretion, but you should be particularly mindful of your target and what lies beyond, and be aware that it is a very low-percentage shot, with a high probability of missed or wounded game.

which offer comparable ballistics to magnums, with less recoil.

Some of you may have noticed that I have not mentioned the venerable .30-30 up to this point. If you look at a ballistic chart, it is not a particularly good choice for deer. However, I'd venture to guess that more deer have been killed with this caliber than any other. This only serves to emphasize the point that the shooter is far more important than the gun.

Whatever caliber or action you choose, you should be proficient with your firearm. You need to know its strengths and limitations and understand that higher velocity and energy are no substitute for good marksmanship and careful shot placement.

Bullets

The primary function of big-game bullets is to expand gradually as the bullet impacts and penetrates: controlled expansion. How much and how quickly a bullet expands can vary considerably with bullet types. The basic design is a lead core with a copper jacket. The thinner the jacket, the more rapidly the bullet will expand or mushroom. Faster expansion can also be facilitated in several ways. One is simply to expose the lead core at the bullet's tip, as in Remington's pointed soft-point bullets. Another is to add a harder, nonexpanding tip, as in Winchester's ballistic-tip bullets. More complicated designs such as the Nosler partition and Swift A-frame have separate chambers, front and back, so the front expands while the rear remains intact and drives the bullet forward.

Before it can expand, however, you have to deliver the bullet to its target, which requires aerodynamics. Deer bullets can be divided into two basic shapes. The most common is the spitzer (German for "pointed"), which has a better aerodynamic shape and thus is good for medium- to long-range shots. The other, the round-nosed bullet, is a better choice for shorter ranges and thick cover. It's less aerodynamic, but a broader tip with more exposed lead hastens expansion. A slight variation of the spitzer is the boat tail. Its tapered base reduces air drag, offering improved aerodynamics. As a result, the bullet retains more velocity and energy for a flatter trajectory and more energy, making it a better choice for long-range shots.

Style

This brings up an important point. Often your intended use will dictate the best overall rifle choice. Someone sitting in a shooting house in Texas or over a food plot in Alabama—long-range shots at a relatively stationary target—may want a longer, heavier-barreled, bolt-action rifle in a flat-shooting caliber like the .270, 7mm Remington magnum, .300 Win mag, or .300 WSM. A mountain rifle offers a similar configuration in a more compact, portable package—shorter barrel, lighter stock. Still hunters and the legendary deer trackers of the north woods generally prefer a shorter-barreled, lighter repeater such as the pump, semiauto, or lever action. They also prefer a heavier caliber and bullet, such as the 150-grain .30-30 or the 180-grain .308 or .30-06. Single-shot, break-action rifles have also become more popular in recent years. I'm not quite sure why, but I suspect it has something to do with outdoor television shows and advertising.

Shotguns

There was a time, not so long ago, when those intending to hunt deer with a shotgun merely loaded their favorite fowling piece with buckshot or "pumpkin balls." With the dramatic increase in suburban sprawl, and its associated firearms restrictions, shotguns have become increasingly popular among deer hunters. Gun makers responded to the increased demand first with improved ammunition for smoothbores and later with rifled barrels designed specifically for hunting deer and other large game. Nowadays many slug guns

■ Many states now restrict deer hunters to shotguns only. Fortunately, with modern slug guns and ammunition, you can achieve riflelike accuracy, albeit at shorter ranges.

claim riflelike accuracy, albeit at somewhat shorter ranges. A select few actually accomplish it.

Action

You can find slug guns in all the same actions as rifles, though lever actions are few and far between. Newer bolt actions offer the greatest accuracy, primarily because the barrel and action are integrated into a single piece. Some of the better break actions offer similar accuracy when a scope is mounted on the barrel. Pumps and autoloaders are the most

popular and offer the greatest range of choices. However, in conventional models the scope is mounted to the receiver, which is a separate piece from the barrel. You can increase accuracy by selecting a slug gun with a cantilever scope mount, where the scope is mounted to the barrel rather than to the receiver.

Gauge

Most of the innovations in slug guns have been in 12 gauge, which is probably your best option anyway. Smaller guns, in 20 gauge, may be a better option for younger or smaller-framed hunters, but they lack the effective range and knockdown power of a 12. More than a few youngsters have probably killed their first deer with a .410, but a 20 gauge is a far more effective and therefore ethical choice. The .410 is somewhat akin to a golf club. You can kill a deer with it if you can get close enough.

Chamber

Within the 12-gauge realm, you can choose from 2¾-, 3-, and 3½-inch chamber lengths, the latter of which are designed to accommodate larger loads. The larger, magnum loads allow for more powder and heavier projectiles. As all loads can be fired from guns chambered for 3½ inches, this offers the greatest versatility. However, bigger is not necessarily better, and every gun will perform differently with different loads. Before you hunt, you should try several different loads to see which your gun shoots best.

Loads

Speaking of loads, you have two general choices. Far and away the most popular are slug guns, which are designed to be shot like a rifle, by aiming at a particular point and shooting at a (hopefully) stationary target. They can be either rifled or smoothbore. Rifled slug guns are a much better option; they're designed for slugs and are far more accurate. Nowadays most hunters who still use smoothbores either use their slug gun for other game as well or can't afford a new slug gun. An economical option is to simply buy a rifled slug barrel for your all-purpose shotgun.

In terms of slug (bullet) type, hunters have a broad range to choose from. Considerable attention has been paid in recent years to designing slugs to be more like rifle bullets. Hollow points allow for

■ A simple, 1x red-dot scope can enhance short-range target acquisition on your slug gun.
COURTESY OF MANUFACTURER

greater expansion, while copper-alloy jackets control that expansion. Saboted slugs allow you to shoot a lighter projectile, which means greater speed and flatter trajectory. As the name implies, smoothbores lack rifling, so you need a rifled slug. Rifled slugs are not recommended for use in rifled slug barrels as the rifling of slug and barrel may be incompatible, which could significantly affect bullet flight.

Slug guns are inherently less accurate. Part of the reason for that is the extreme disparity in slug diameters. Commercial slug-barrel makers have to compensate for that by designing barrels that will accommodate the largest-diameter slugs. As a result, anything smaller will not properly seat in the rifling. Some of the more recent saboted slugs, like Lightfield's Hybred, are designed to expand within the barrel to engage rifling, regardless of internal bore diameter.

Unlike slugs, buckshot is more of a point-and-shoot load, designed to cover

■ Ammunition manufacturers have kept pace with the increased popularity and accuracy of slug guns by developing slugs designed specifically for rifled barrels.

the general target area with a pattern of shot. It is considerably less accurate and only has an effective range of about 40 yards. Again, it only has an effective range of about 40 yards. That's worth repeating for emphasis. You can kill deer beyond this range with buckshot—if you're lucky. Far more often, shots over 40 yards result in either clean misses or deer that are wounded and lost. Still, for close hunting in very dense cover, or with youth hunters, buckshot may offer some advantages.

Handguns

Handguns represent a sort of specialty group among deer hunters and are typically used by those who prefer the superior ballistics of centerfire cartridges but are looking for more of a challenge. With the heavier calibers needed for deer hunting, you're largely limited to revolvers or single-shot, break-action guns, with the latter being heavily favored. Heavy-caliber revolvers such as the .41 and .44 magnum have the power and trajectory for shots out to 100 yards. Conversely, many of the more common break-action types are available in the gamut of deer-hunting calibers, from .243 Win. up to .45-70 Government.

Muzzleloaders

There are two primary differences between muzzleloaders and other "modern" firearms. First, as the name implies, muzzleloaders are loaded through the

■ **Advancements in modern muzzleloaders have prompted many deer hunters to take up the added challenge of hunting with a smokepole. The accuracy of in-line muzzleloaders with telescopic sights can now rival that of centerfire rifles out to 100 yards or more.** COURTESY OF MANUFACTURER

muzzle rather than the breech. Second, rather than an integrated, enclosed shotshell or cartridge, the components of your loads are separate.

Like shotguns, muzzleloaders that are designed specifically for deer hunting have improved dramatically in recent years. The greatest change has been from traditional side-hammer mechanisms to in-line ignition systems, which tend to be more accurate and significantly more reliable. Some hunters still favor the nostalgia of traditional styles, and they are mandatory in some primitive firearms seasons. However, if your goal is a quick, clean kill, in-lines offer a better option, where allowed.

Action

General action types or ignition systems basically include flintlock and caplock, in the primitive category, and bolt or break action in the in-lines. Caplocks offer a more reliable ignition system than flintlocks, but some hunters prefer the nostalgia of the more primitive flintlock. With the in-lines, break actions are becoming more popular, as they are easier to operate and clean. Many are now built so the ignition system—often a .209 shotgun primer—is fully enclosed so it is protected from the elements.

Caliber

For deer hunting .50 caliber is the standard among muzzleloaders, with options ranging from .45 to .56. Lighter bullets have a flatter trajectory but less energy. The most common load is a .50 caliber with 100 grains (more or less) of powder. However, with stronger barrels and pellets, more shooters are going to .45 caliber bullets with 130 to 150 grains of powder. This offers a flatter trajectory than a .50 caliber bullet, and the increased speed makes up for any lost kinetic energy. Some hunters prefer heavier bullets in .54 or even .56

caliber, particularly those shooting loose powder in caplocks and flintlocks.

You can significantly improve the effectiveness of your muzzleloader by fine-tuning your bullet/powder combination. If you're using loose powder, start at the low end— 80 to 90 grains—and work up. A heavy load of 130 or 150 grains might sound better, but you may find your gun shoots best at around 100, and any more is just a waste. You should also try several different bullet types to see which one groups best.

Powder

Formerly, loose powder was the only way to go and still is with flintlock and caplock muzzleloaders. But pellets offer a more efficient and convenient option for in-lines. Some of the newer types of both powder and pellets are also designed to burn cleaner, for faster and easier cleanup.

Bullets

There are almost as many choices in muzzleloader bullets as in centerfire bullets and maybe more types than shotgun slugs. Each has the same advantages and disadvantages as the aforementioned types, and the best way to determine which is best for you is to try several.

Few hunters now use smoothbore muzzleloaders, but for those that do, a patched round ball is the best choice in projectiles. Saboted bullets offer the advantage of a faster, lighter projectile, which means greater effective range and less lead and copper fouling of your barrel.

Again, you need to fine-tune your loads, especially when using sabots. Most in-lines have an unrifled loading cone at the muzzle end of the barrel, where the sabot will expand. Too little or too much powder will result in too little or too much expansion, which can affect accuracy.

Possibles

Another major difference between breech loaders and muzzleloaders is that with the latter you'll also need some additional equipment, commonly referred to as possibles. This includes a nipple or breech-plug wrench and nipple pick for disassembling and cleaning the ignition system. You can speed up your reloading time by carrying premeasured powder and shot charges in airtight "speed-loader" capsules, and by using a capping tool, preloaded with caps or primers. You'll also need a ball or bullet starter to get your projectile started down the muzzle, before you switch to a ramrod.

Sights

The three basic sight types are open, peep, and telescopic, and within those is a range of options. Basic, open sights are simple and virtually maintenance free, once they're sighted in. On the minus side, they're generally less accurate and better suited to short-range shooting. Their effectiveness can be enhanced by using fiber optic versions, which make sight acquisition easier, particularly in low-light conditions.

Some hunters feel peep sights offer better sight acquisition and accuracy and may be better suited to still-hunting, particularly in dense cover or inclement weather.

Far and away the most popular type is telescopic sights, or optics. The simplest, more often used on shotguns, lack magnification and use an illuminated red dot, or holographic reticle, in the center of the scope.

Most hunters, both shotgunners and rifle hunters, prefer some sort of magnification, and just as with caliber and bullet weight, the right choice may depend on how or where you hunt. In general, as you increase magnification, you reduce the field of view. You also increase the effect of motion. High-power scopes are better suited to long-range shooting, where magnification becomes more important, and you usually have a solid rest. Low

■ One of the biggest mistakes hunters make is buying an expensive rifle, then putting a cheap scope on it. In low-light conditions, quality optics can often make the difference between success and failure.

power is better for short-range shooting, especially when still-hunting in thick cover, where quick target acquisition may be more important.

Variable scopes offer greater versatility. You can crank your scope down to 4x when still-hunting your way to your stand. Then, once you're situated, crank it back up to 6x. And when that bruiser buck steps into the food plot out at 150 yards, boost it up to 9x.

If you use optics, don't scrimp. I've queried numerous guides and outfitters on mistakes deer hunters make, and one of the most often cited is buying cheap optics. Hunters will spend $500 to $700 on a rifle, then buy a $150 scope.

The biggest difference between cheap and expensive scopes is the glass. High-quality glass is costly, and on a bright, sunny day, or in the gun shop, you may not notice the difference. However, in low-light conditions at twilight, when you're most likely to need it, the improved light transmission of high-quality optics more than pays for itself.

Accessories and Options

There are a few accessories you may want to add on to your firearm. One of the most obvious is a sling. It offers an alternative means for carrying your gun. Wrapping your forearm in the sling when shooting also offers a steadier shooting platform. You can get an even steadier platform by using shooting sticks or a bipod. Sticks are usually carried separately, while a bipod is often fixed to the stock.

Speaking of stocks, you have several choices there as well. First, there's the traditional wood stock. Real traditionalists can choose from attractive hardwoods such as walnut and maple, typically with a high-gloss finish. It's attractive, but it reflects sunlight and mars easily. Or you can choose a dull, matte-finish hardwood stock, like birch. Laminated wood stocks offer good looks with greater durability. They're also somewhat more stable than straight wood stocks, which can swell and shrink with changes in moisture and temperature. This in turn can affect accuracy. At the other end are synthetic stocks. They're generally considered less attractive but are the most durable, sturdy, stable, and lightweight.

Sighting In

Before you can hunt, you need to make sure your firearm is sighted in so it is shooting accurately. If you have your scope mounted by a gun shop, they'll usually bore sight it for you. This will at least get you close enough to begin the process on your own. From a solid rest, carefully squeeze off three aimed shots. This group will determine your current point of impact.

Now you can adjust the scope reticle, or sights, according to how the point of impact differs from the point of aim. With open sights move your sights in the same direction you want your group to move. For example, if you're hitting three inches low, adjust your rear sight up. Similarly, if your point of impact is left of the point of aim, move your rear sight to the right.

The process is somewhat easier with scopes. Most scopes come with graduated adjustment knobs that indicate the range and direction of adjustment; e.g., one click equals ¼ inch of adjustment at 100 yards. There should also be an arrow on the adjustment knob that will indicate which way you are moving your group.

Continue this process until your group is where you want it. Don't make adjustments based on a single shot, as odd shots can lead to adjustment errors and wasted time and ammunition. Also, sight your gun in with the same ammunition you will hunt with, as different brands, bullet weights, and types will shoot differently.

Where you want your group can depend on several things. If most of your shooting will be at 100 yards or under, you can simply sight in for 100 yards. If you're shooting at longer ranges, you may want to sight in so you're hitting a few inches high at 100 yards. In order to determine how high, you'll need to consult a ballistics and trajectory chart. This will help you decide where the optimum point of impact is for your load and intended use.

Cleaning and Practice

Two other mistakes that hunters often make are not cleaning their guns and not

■ Practice shooting enough so that you are familiar and proficient with your gun. Shoot it before you hunt as well, to ensure your sights are still on.

practicing with them. At the very least, you should clean your gun at the end of every season. Run a solvent-soaked patch down the barrel and let it sit for a while to dissolve lead, copper, and powder fouling. Then run dry patches through until they come out clean. Finally, run a patch lightly soaked with oil down the barrel, clean and oil the working parts, and it's ready for storage.

Before you hunt again, it's a good idea to fire a round, as heavy oil residue could affect accuracy.

You should fire your gun at the range before you hunt anyway. Lots of things can happen over the course of the season. Your gun could get bumped getting in and out of the truck or up and down from your stand. Don't assume just because your gun was on last year that it still is this year; you could be sorely disappointed.

CHAPTER THREE

Archery Tackle

Bowhunting differs from gun hunting in several ways. Aside from the obvious distance limitations, one of the biggest differences is the equipment. The bowhunter uses not just a bow but a shooting system, consisting of bow, arrows, and accessories; each component must be fitted appropriately and fine-tuned to the shooter because the shooter is also part of the system.

■ By opting to use a bow, the hunter not only places greater challenges upon himself, but creates both a need and an opportunity to learn more about the whitetail.

The basis for the system is the bow itself. Just as you need to know your shoe size when selecting hunting boots, you need to know your individual draw length when choosing a bow. You also need to know whether you're a left- or right-hand shooter (see Determining Your Dominant Eye on page 25).

Draw Length

Your first consideration is draw length—a measurement from the forward face of the bow riser grip to the nock point, when the bow is held at full draw. Your best bet is to go to the local pro shop and have them measure you. However, you can also measure your draw length at home, with a tape measure and a helper (see Measuring Draw Length on page 25). You'll also need to determine whether you plan on shooting with fingers or a release aid, as the latter will require a slightly shorter draw length.

Draw Weight

Your next consideration is draw weight—a measure of the maximum number of pounds weight you must pull in order to bring the bow to full draw. Most modern

DETERMINING YOUR DOMINANT EYE

Incidentally, before you determine whether you're a right-hand or left-hand shooter, you should determine which is your dominant eye. If you're right-handed, but left-eye dominant, you may actually find it easier to shoot left-handed.

Determining your dominant eye is done as follows. With both eyes open, extend your arm and point your index finger at an object roughly 10 feet away. Now close your left eye. If your finger is still pointing at the object, you're right-eye dominant. Open both eyes; then close your right eye. Your finger should now be pointing to the right of the object. If the reverse is true, you're left-eye dominant.

compounds have eccentric cams, so you'll actually achieve maximum weight before you come to full draw (more on that later).

How many pounds you need is nearly as contentious an issue as what caliber is best for deer. Many states have specific minimum weights if you intend to shoot large game—40 pounds is common. This is enough to kill a deer, but you may want more weight for larger game, such as bear, moose, and elk. More weight also means greater arrow speed, flatter trajectory, more kinetic energy, and potentially greater penetration. Most adult

MEASURING DRAW LENGTH

I'll use the example of a right-handed shooter (reverse directions if you're left-handed). Stand sideways toward a wall, with your bow (left) hand facing the wall, in the same posture as if you were going to shoot a bow toward the wall. Make a fist and extend your bow arm toward the wall until the flat face of your knuckles is flush against the wall. Now step back until your arm is out straight.

Don't try to overextend your arm. It should be out relatively straight. You'll know if you're overextending because the inside of your elbow joint will begin to jut outward where, if you were actually shooting a bow, it might get slapped by the bowstring upon release. Next, turn your head and face the wall. Then, with a tape measure, have someone measure the distance between the wall and the right corner of your mouth. This distance is your draw length.

It's also important to know whether or not you intend to shoot with fingers (a shooting glove or a tab) or with a release aid, before you actually go out and buy a bow. When shooting with gloved fingers or a tab, you'll probably want a bow in your exact draw length. Depending on where you decide to anchor (more on that in a moment), a release aid can add ½ to 1 inch to your draw length, so you may want a bow that is ½ to 1 inch shorter than your measured or actual draw length.

bowhunters probably pull between 60 and 70 pounds.

It's important to bear in mind that greater speed can also mean reduced accuracy if your shooting form is not perfect. The faster your bow is, the more it will exaggerate minor breakdowns in shooting form. This is less of a problem for the target shooter and more of a problem for the hunter, who may have to shoot from odd angles or positions, all of which change your form.

More weight is also harder to draw. Another consideration for the hunter is muscle atrophy. Shooting on the range in 65-degree Fahrenheit temperature, you may be able to pull 75 pounds all day long. But sit in your treestand for four or five hours when the mercury is hovering around the freezing mark and then try to draw it back, especially after your muscles are already twitching from that sudden surge of adrenaline when old Harvey Wall-hanger suddenly steps into view. That's why you should pick a weight you can draw comfortably, under a range of conditions.

Bear in mind that, as you practice, you'll build up your shooting muscles and soon will be able to pull more weight. Also, you can adjust the draw weight on nearly all compound bows simply by turning the limb bolts. Many bowhunters will begin their preseason practice at lower draw weights, then crank up the pounds as they rebuild shooting muscles.

So what's the right weight? Again, that depends largely on the shooter. Sixty to 70 pounds is probably a good range for an average adult male. Women, youths, and smaller-framed adults may do better in the 50- to 55-pound range. With plenty of practice, 70 to 75 pounds is reasonable for a stronger shooter. Beyond that, if you can shoot it comfortably and consistently, even under extreme conditions, go for it.

Let-Off

Yet another option you have when choosing a compound is percent let-off. The first compounds came with round wheels, so you pulled the same weight from start to finish and had to hold the full weight until you shot. Now, cams are shaped eccentrically. Toward the end of your draw, the wheels "break over" and *let off* some of the draw weight. Options in let-off range roughly from 65 to 80 percent. The advantage to higher let-off is obvious: you're holding less weight at full draw so you can hold longer.

Most modern compound bows now come standard with 80 to 85 percent let-off, with the option of 65 percent. Since the Pope and Young Club has begun accepting trophies taken with bows higher than 65 percent let-off, that trend is likely to continue, with lower let-off becoming even less common.

Cams

In recent years the most innovations in bows have come with regard to cams. As

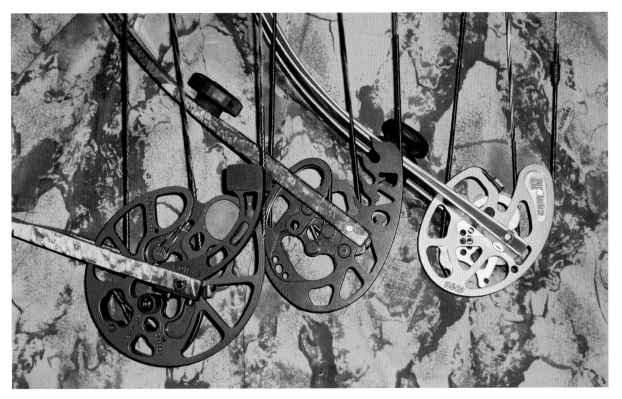

■ Bowhunters now have a broad array of cams to choose from, depending on their needs and preferences. Pictured here are (left to right) Mathews Straightline HP Cam, Renegade Archery RAC1 Cam, and Hoyt Cam &½.

mentioned earlier, the first compounds came with round wheels. Later, with more eccentric cams, bows became faster and offered greater let-off. However, in order to achieve consistent accuracy, both cams must turn over at precisely the same time, and as bowstrings stretch with age, hard-cam bows can go out of tune more easily. If the cams are out of time, the first cam starts to move and the second cam has to catch up. This causes a bump in the nock and poor arrow flight.

One of the first solutions to this was the so-called one-cam bow. It has one round wheel and one eccentrically shaped wheel. The round wheel is always turning consistently. So theoretically, the bow cannot

go out of tune if the string stretches. The only downside to one-cam bows, if there is one, is that they typically have a very eccentric cam, for speed, and thus have a less smooth pull. Most also have a let-off greater than 65 percent.

A more recent innovation is the cam and a half or hybrid cam. Like the original two-cam bows, the system incorporates two cams that are identical, top and bottom. The difference is in the modules. Unlike the two-cam system, where both modules are also identical, the cam and a half utilizes two different modules. The bottom one is the same as on a two-cam. The top module is round and lacks a stop. This allows it to rotate immediately from any position at the same time as the bottom cam. In addition, the cam-and-a-half system has a different yoke-and-cable system that helps eliminate timing problems and a fitted ball bearing system to help reduce cam lean and the resultant cable wear.

It should also be noted that many cams come with multiple slots or removable modules. This allows you to fine-tune the bow's draw length to the individual shooter's draw length in ½-inch increments. It also allows you to readjust if you change anchor points, release aids, etc. The range of adjustment varies between bows from approximately 2 inches to 5 inches. Those with larger ranges may be a better choice for younger shooters, as they won't outgrow their bows quite so fast.

Brace Height

Yet another measurement you should consider when selecting a bow is brace height. This is the perpendicular distance between the bowstring and the grip of the riser handle. Longer brace heights tend to be more forgiving than shorter ones, which can exaggerate minor breakdowns in shooting form, especially torque. It's difficult to explain in simple terms, but torque is what happens when you grip, rather than hold, the bow. The harder you grip it, the more the bow torques to one side, leading to inaccuracy. Longer brace height means there is more arrow behind the torque point rather than in front of it, and the effects are lessened.

■ Increasingly, bow manufacturers are shifting toward parallel limbs. The closer the top and bottom limbs are to being parallel with one another, the more they cancel out shock and vibration.

Limbs

While it has little bearing on fit, another option when choosing a new compound is limb type. There are essentially two from which to choose: solid and split. Solid means that each of the two bow limbs consists of a single piece. In the case of a split-limb bow, both top and bottom limbs actually consist of two separate pieces. The split limb, a relatively recent innovation, was originally intended as an answer to occasional stress fractures in solid limbs, and as a way to reduce bow weight. One drawback is that they have a slightly higher incidence of cam lean. Advancements in limb construction technology have all but eliminated cracks and stress fractures, however, and the current trend is moving back toward solid limbs.

Models

With so many models to choose from, your toughest choice may be selecting the model that's right for you. Nowadays bowhunters have more choices than ever, and as with computers, technological advancements continue to drive prices down. Modern compounds might seem more expensive, but when you consider how much more efficient and effective they are compared to ten years ago, they're a relative bargain.

Accessories

The second leg of our shooting system triad is accessories—everything else you put on the bow to make it shoot well.

Rests

Rests are not as important for the instinctive shooter, but they are crucial to bow performance for the twenty-first-century competitive compound shooter or the hunter looking for the most technologically efficient killing machine he can build. They must be precisely tuned to counteract flexing of the arrow shaft that results when the bowstring is released, whether you're shooting fingers or release. They

■ Archers can choose from several styles of arrow rests, including (top to bottom) (1) drop away (Muzzy Zero Effect), (2) flipper (NAP QuickTune), and (3) capture (CAP Whisker Biscuit).

must be adjustable to accept differently spined arrows, and serious archers and tinkerers alike insist that these adjustments be precise and minute for fine-tuning.

The most common type is the shoot-through rest, where the arrow shaft is held on a set of prongs or launchers, usually coated with Teflon or some other durable, noise-free material. A more recent innovation is the drop-away rest. When the string is released, the launchers drop away so there is no contact between shaft and rest, meaning less noise, friction, and influence on arrow flight. Another popular type is the biscuit or disk. Rather than resting on a pair of launchers, the arrow shaft is encircled with a synthetic material that will hold it in place but will let it pass through at the shot. There is more contact between shaft, fletching, and rest, but the arrow cannot fall off the rest.

Sights

When it comes to sights, you have a ton of choices, but there are some basic guidelines that can help you narrow down which is best for you. Your first decision will be whether you want a fixed or adjustable sight, and this is largely a matter of personal preference. Fixed sights use multiple pins for various distances. The pins can be initially adjustable for sighting in but then remain fixed in an unmovable housing. Adjustable sights generally use a single pin mounted in a movable bracket. The shooter compensates for various distances by moving the entire sight assembly up or down,

■ One of the keys to being a successful bowhunter is to practice with the equipment you will hunt with. This includes shooting broadheads and wearing your hunting clothes. COURTESY OF MANUFACTURER

and on some models this can even be done while at full draw. Pendulum sights consist of a single pin mounted on a pendulum. As you lower or raise your bow, the pendulum swings up or down, automatically adjusting for distance. These types are designed specifically for the treestand hunter.

Your next choice is pin type. For hunting you should consider nothing less than fiber optic pins. The introduction of Tru-Glo fibers was one of the milestones in modern archery accessories, and few, if any, contemporary sights come without fiber optic pins. In daylight they aren't all that impressive, but during those crucial fifteen to twenty minutes of twilight, when most deer are moving and most deer are shot, they make a world of difference. Two more recent innovations are a glow ring around the sight aperture, to aid in twilight target and pin acquisition, and tritium pins, which can actually store ambient light and emit it in darker periods.

A good hunting sight needs to be rugged in order to hold up to the rigors of hunting: repeated raising and lowering from a treestand, bulling through brush, or simple day-to-day transportation to and from the woods. It should be made of tough material that will hold up to both the elements and the conditions under which it's used. Plastic breaks, soft metal bends, and steel rusts, so polycarbonate, aluminum, and stainless steel are better choices. Your sight should have some sort of pin guard to protect the delicate sight pins and transparent or translucent guards to allow more light in.

Finally, hunting sights need to be versatile. Discriminating bowhunters want a sight they can adjust precisely, while many average archers are more concerned with one that's easy to adjust. The best ones can be adjusted in the field with few if any tools, while retaining precision.

Shock and Noise

When you release your bowstring, most of the stored energy is transferred to your

■ Vibration- and noise-dampening technology can be attached at numerous locations including the string, limbs, limb pockets, riser, and cable guard rod. In some cases even sights, rests, and quivers come with dampening now.

arrow. The rest is dissipated through the bow as vibration and as noise. A lot more attention is being paid nowadays to reducing bow noise and vibration. One way is by attaching some sort of silencer to your string. Another is by attaching shock absorbers to your limbs and riser. A stabilizer, which is attached to your riser, not only helps balance the bow but absorbs excess shock and noise. These are all commonly available accessories, but more and more bows are available with these as integral parts.

Release Aids

A release aid is actually more a part of the shooter than the bow. It is a device, usually some type of caliper, that attaches to the bowstring or string loop. It has certain advantages over shooting with fingers. One is that the string is pulled directly back and upon release moves directly forward. Conversely, shooting with fingers tends to roll the string, resulting in less consistent accuracy.

Which type you should choose will depend on several things, including personal preference. Some hunters prefer a release that straps onto their wrist, so it's always there when they need it. Others prefer a more compact type that they merely hold in their hand, so they can put it in their pocket or out of the way when they don't need it.

The best way to select a release is to go to your local pro shop and try several out until you find one you are comfortable with. A release aid will add more expense to your initial investment but will ultimately make you a better shooter.

Arrows and Broadheads

The third part of our shooting system is the arrow-broadhead combination. Your bow's specifications will dictate, to a large extent, what size arrow you can use. Length should match your draw length, and spine (relative stiffness) will be determined by this, draw weight, and point weight. You can easily determine the right size by consulting an arrow-selection chart.

Your biggest choice will be in shaft material. Some traditional shooters still

■ Arrow shafts are available in aluminum, aluminum/carbon composite, or all carbon. Whatever you choose, make sure the arrow is properly spined for your bow.

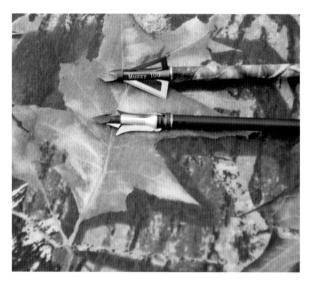

■ The two basic types of broadheads are fixed (Muzzy 100) and mechanical (Grim Reaper Razortip).

use wooden arrows, usually cedar, but many prefer aluminum. Once the favorite of compound shooters, more recently, aluminum has all but been replaced by carbon or aluminum-carbon arrows. Carbon and carbon-alloy shafts help complement the trend in faster, flatter-shooting bows by providing a rugged, durable, and aerodynamically precise projectile. Carbon technology also allows arrow makers to produce stronger, straighter, and rounder shafts with continually diminishing tolerances for straightness and variability between individual arrows.

Broadheads are analogous to bullets, as they are what actually inflicts the wound. And there is an ever-increasing field to choose from.

The two major types are fixed and mechanical (expandable). There is considerable debate over which type is best, and each has pluses and minuses. The major advantage of mechanicals is that arrow flight is nearly the same as with field or practice heads, while fixed heads may require additional tuning and sight adjustment. One disadvantage is that mechanical heads may take up to 15 foot-pounds of energy just to open, leaving less energy for penetration. Once open, they create a larger wound, but the energy loss reduces the likelihood of a complete pass-through. Fixed heads, on the other hand, tend to provide greater penetration and are more durable.

There are myriad options in terms of blade shape, size, configuration, and materials. Some heads use a chisel tip for bone-breaking durability, while others are full-bladed for better cutting. Most have rugged, stainless steel blades. Three-bladed models allegedly offer slightly better flight, while four blades offer more cutting surface. Removable blades offer an economical replacement option while nonremovable blades tend to be stronger.

They also come in various weights, generally 85, 100, and 125 grains. Heavier heads store more energy but also add weight, which reduces speed. The trade-off is nearly equal.

Crossbows

No summary of modern archery equipment would be complete without some mention of crossbows. As wildlife managers struggle to find ways to attract more deer hunters and reduce problem-deer numbers, crossbows are becoming legal hunting weapons in an ever-growing list of states.

There are a few differences between crossbows and compound bows. The limbs of the crossbow are held horizontally rather than vertically, and the string of a crossbow is mechanically held in the full-draw position. Hunting crossbows require a higher draw weight—usually in the 150-pound range—to compensate for a much shorter axle-to-axle length (roughly 22 inches compared to a compound's average of 40 inches). The resulting energy and effective range is quite similar to that of a compound bow.

■ Crossbows are being legalized for hunting in an ever-growing list of states. Their use may enable wildlife managers to attract more deer hunters and reduce problem-deer numbers.

In a side-by-side comparison, the compound bow actually has a slight advantage over the crossbow. Because they shoot a lighter projectile (called a bolt), crossbows have a more curved trajectory. Likewise, energy and velocity losses escalate faster than with the heavier arrows used in compounds. Thus, range estimation is more critical within the same effective range. Most crossbow manufacturers recommend a maximum effective range of 40 yards.

Furthermore, the heavier arrows have a better penetration rate than the lighter bolts, particularly at increasing ranges. Also, crossbows are noisier at the shot, increasing the potential for a deer to "jump the string," particularly at longer ranges.

One advantage to crossbows is that they are easier to learn to shoot. The sighting system is more like that of a rifle, in that, once sighted in, the crossbow can be used by different individuals. While a basic crossbow might come with open or peep sights, some can be fitted with scopes. In that case, it's a good idea to have a scope with graduated reticles to compensate for yardage differences.

And one more advantage to crossbows is that they require fewer accessories. Sights, a quiver, and perhaps a sling are about all you need to add. The bolts are fairly universal, and you can use the same broadheads you use on your compound bow.

Conclusion

So there you have it. If it still seems too complicated and confusing, don't despair. All you really need to be concerned with are draw length and how much draw weight you can comfortably pull. Your local pro shop can help you with the rest. Again, the key is to find a bow you can shoot comfortably, as confidence is also an important part of your shooting system. Pick good-quality accessories that fit your needs and preferences. Then select the right shaft and broadhead combination, and you're ready to start shooting.

Before you go afield, though, you need to practice with field tips until you are proficient, then switch to broadheads to fine-tune your equipment. If you hunt from an elevated stand, practice from one. Wear the same clothes you'll be hunting with, especially headwear and face mask.

■ Selecting the right equipment and fine-tuning it so you are shooting accurately and consistently are important steps toward your bowhunting success.

CHAPTER FOUR

Treestands, Towers, and Ground Blinds

It's a fairly safe assumption that the vast majority of deer hunters prefer to hunt from a fixed location, at least part of the time. This is especially true for bowhunters. Doing so has certain advantages, which we'll cover in a later chapter. In order to do so effectively however, you need to be both comfortable and concealed, and you can go a long way from wearing a camo coat and sitting on a tree stump. The most popular way is to use an elevated stand, which includes both free-standing stands and treestands.

Next to your gun or bow and perhaps optics, a stand (or stands) will likely be your most expensive equipment investment. You want something that you'll be happy with, that will suit your needs, and that will last through your lifetime of deer hunting. That's why it's worth examining all available options. In this chapter we'll take a collective look at the various stand types available. And for those who prefer to keep their feet firmly on the ground, we'll also look at earthbound means of concealment.

■ Elevating one's self above the eyes, ears, and nose of the whitetail offers some distinct advantages over hunting from the ground.

Treestands

Treestands generally come in three different configurations: fixed-position (FPS) or hang-on, climbers, and ladders. Each has its particular applications, advantages, and disadvantages.

In all cases there are certain basic considerations. One is material. Steel stands tend to be less expensive but are heavier, and they rust. Aluminum is lighter but more expensive.

Another consideration is capacity. Most modern stands have a minimum capacity of about 200 pounds, with larger, single-person stands ranging up to 350 pounds. Some dual stands have capacities of as much as 500 pounds. If you're a big person, hunt with a buddy or a kid, or prefer the added security (and often room), go with a bigger stand.

It's worth noting that almost any treestand today is an incredible value. The technology, materials, and construction have improved exponentially, yet prices have remained relatively stable. For almost the same price you can buy double the stand you could ten years ago.

Ladders

Ladders are best suited to situations where you plan to erect them well in advance of your hunt and leave them there for some time. That's because they're heavy and bulky and they require a good deal of effort to erect. However, once installed they provide a stable and often spacious platform. They can also be used in some

■ **Ladders are best suited to situations where you plan to erect them well in advance of your hunt and leave them there for some time.** COURTESY OF MANUFACTURER

situations where other types cannot (for example, in smaller trees).

Options run the gamut from a basic standing platform to a two-man bench seat. Heights generally range from 10 to 16 feet. Some have a single-ladder unit, while many come in 3- or 4-foot sections for greater portability, with the option to make them taller. Some ladders have a single rail, while others have a heavier but more stable double rail.

Platforms and seats are usually made of expanded steel, which keeps them light yet stable. You can add a padded seat and back rest for comfort, though these often come as standard equipment. Some have an enclosed safety rail, which doubles as a shooting rail. Bowhunters might prefer one with an open front. If you want one stand for both seasons, you can get one with a removable or fold-up shooting rail. Some even have seats that will fold up and out of the way for standing.

One innovative model, API's Packmaster, bridges the gap between ladders and hang-ons. It's a mobile ladder, fixed-position platform, and telescoping ladder all in one. The telescoping ladder extends to a seat height of 17 feet and can be folded down into a compact package that can easily be carried like a backpack, both in minutes.

Fixed-Position Stands

FPSs represent a sort of middle ground between ladders and climbers and are better suited to semipermanent locations—situations where you hang them well in advance of your hunt, leave them in place, and perhaps don't plan on hunting as long. They are much easier to transport and install than ladders but lack the comfort and security of a larger platform. They're generally lighter and slightly more portable than climbers but require more effort (and usually noise) to install.

SAFETY

The leading cause of injury among hunters is falling from an elevated position (stand). One very simple way to avoid this is always to wear a safety harness when hunting from a stand. Thanks to a cooperative effort by the Treestand Manufacturer's Association, all TMA-certified stands are now sold with a full-body fall-restraint device.

WEAR IT. And if you don't have one, BUY ONE. The expense and inconvenience of buying and wearing a full-body harness are minor compared to what could happen if you fall. Even if you survive, you could be permanently disabled.

Besides, not only will it keep you safe, it can reduce noise. The sounds of your yelling as you fall to the ground, crashing when you hit, and screaming as you writhe in pain on the forest floor are certain to spook deer.

■ Fixed-position stands provide a more portable option than ladders but are still best installed in advance of your hunt. COURTESY OF MANUFACTURER

Like the other types, they come in an array of shapes and sizes. The basic concept is a platform and a seat, which you attach to a tree. They attach with either a hook and chain or a ratchet strap, and some models feature both. Some models also feature a mounting-bracket system that allows the hunter to utilize multiple locations with a single stand. While most require that you must climb up to or slightly above the stand to enter, at least one type features a bottom-entry design.

Seats

The greatest range of options is found in seats. Fold-out or cloth or web sling seats are the simplest, lightest, and usually the least expensive but also the least comfortable. Seats that are suspended from the sides rather than back to front are slightly more comfortable, as they lack the front bar, which can reduce circulation to the lower extremities.

Padded seats add expense and weight but also comfort. And they come in a range of shapes and sizes. Obviously, the

■ Flip-up seats are a nice option, particularly for bowhunters who prefer to shoot standing up. COURTESY OF MANUFACTURER

■ **The three major tree stand types are: ladder (left), climber (center), and fixed-position or hang-on (right).** COURTESY OF MANUFACTURER

larger a seat is, the more comfortable it is. Most are square or rectangular, though some are now triangular, offering better mobility for the bowhunter. Even greater mobility is afforded by swivel seats.

Some seats can be flipped up and out of the way for standing, and detachable seats can be removed between hunts so you can keep them dry and away from gnawing rodents. Adjustable-height seats let you customize height for comfort or individual users. And zippered gear pouches give you a place to store gadgets.

Options/Accessories

Like ladders, FPSs have a range of optional, removable, or flip-up rails and shooting bars, padded backrests, and armrests. Some types even have independent leveling systems for the seat and the platform, to adjust for tree angle. A few even

have accessory mounting systems so you can attach rails, hangers, camo skirt blinds, even artificial limb camouflage. And at least two have axle kits to let you convert your stand into a game carrier.

FPSs also require a means to access them—steps. Tree steps come in an array of forms ranging from simple, screw-in types to full-blown ladders. Screw-ins are the least expensive option. However, they're usually prohibited on public lands, and some landowners would prefer you not use them (always ask first). Fortunately, strap-on steps, which do not damage trees, are also available.

A bulkier, more expensive but more stable and secure option is ladders or climbing sticks. Most come in sections for easier transportation. Some are collapsible or detachable, while others are made up of separate three- or four-step units.

Climbers

Climbers provide for greater flexibility and mobility. You can carry them in, select the right tree, and climb up quickly and quietly in minutes, with minimal effort. They're a little heavier and bulkier than hang-ons, but they offer the advantage of being able to make quick or last-minute changes in your setup location. More than any other type, it seems, treestand makers have gone to great lengths to make climbers more comfortable as well.

The range of options includes size, comfort adjustability, and attachment system. Most utilize some sort of adjustable cable or belt attachment, with the better ones tending to be quieter (reinforced rubber or coated cable) and more rigid. More attention has been given to making the size-adjustment systems quieter and easier to use, with fewer loose pins, knobs, nuts, or bolts to fumble with in the dark and possibly lose. Some stands even feature adjustable leveling systems so you can change your adjustment as you climb to stay level.

Comfort options include padded seats, back and arm rests, and shooting rails. Stands with an open front or removable or convertible rail are a better option for the bowhunter, and like the other types the rails on several climber models can fold out of the way or down to become a footrest. Some stands even fold flat for easy transportation.

Other

It used to be that if you wanted a treestand, you grabbed an armload of 2x4s and some ten-penny nails and built one. Most landowners wouldn't stand for that nowadays, and it's prohibited on public lands. At least one company—Trophyline—offers a neat alternative. The Tree Saddle is essentially a modified lineman's belt—an integrated seat and safety harness you wear in and out.

Freestanding

The least portable but most comfortable stands are tripods and towers. They seem to be far more popular in the South than in the North, perhaps partly because of the longer seasons and greater deer

■ Towers are costly and take a good deal of effort to put up, but they offer the maximum in comfort and concealment.

numbers. They are, however, becoming more popular in all areas where food plots are established. They run the gamut from a simple seat mounted atop three legs to a full-blown, enclosed shooting box on a sturdy tower.

Tower seats are lighter and easier to erect but leave you open to view (unless you add a blind) and the elements. Tower blinds offer the utmost in comfort and concealment. Most are fully enclosed, and some even have windows you can close to shut out the cold.

Ground Blinds

Hunting on the ground has some distinct advantages—mobility, for one. A grounded hunter can pick a spot at random and change locations with a minimum of effort. You also may occasionally find a hot spot that just doesn't lend itself to a stand. However, hunting on the ground also offers certain challenges, especially for the bowhunter. Being at eye level, the hunter becomes more visible.

One of the best ways to overcome this is with a blind, and there are many types to choose from. A simple, makeshift blind can be fashioned from existing vegetation, fallen branches, or an overturned tree. This can be enhanced with a swath of camo material and a handful of clothespins. Or you can build a freestanding blind with camo material and a few old arrow shafts or stakes. Collapsible tent poles provide a more portable alternative, and several companies offer freestanding blinds.

Sometimes a better option is a portable, pop-up blind. These can be carried in and out of the woods like a backpack and set up in seconds. They offer 360 degrees of concealment; some are even made of scent-suppressing material. These blinds also make a handy shelter when you are hunting in inclement weather.

■ Ground blinds have several advantages, including greater mobility and less effort.

CHAPTER FIVE

Dress for Success

As any savvy deer hunter knows, comfort is one of the keys to success. The more comfortable you are, the more time you spend in the woods and the greater your chances of bringing home the venison. And the most important factor in determining how comfortable you are is your apparel. So let's take a head-to-toe look at what you can wear to make you a more successful deer hunter.

Headwear

Starting at the top, you'll need a hat—orange if the law requires it and camo for bowhunting. Choices beyond that

■ What you wear can sometimes be very important to your success. The more comfortable you are, the longer you'll hunt.

■ You can lose up to 80 percent of your body heat through your head, so you'll want a good warm hat for cold conditions and a well-ventilated one when it's warm.

Body Wear

The two keys to effective hunting apparel are layering and moisture management. It's a good idea to dress in layers and err on the side of too much clothing. You can always remove layers, but you can't add them if you don't have them. Moisture management means protecting yourself from environmental moisture (rain and snow) and allowing body moisture to escape.

Mornings on the deer stand often start out cold, just as afternoons end that way. This is where a base layer of long underwear comes in handy. As it's directly against your skin, it should be made of a synthetic material that will wick away perspiration, while providing an extra layer of insulation. Moisture management is also important if you build up a "head of steam" hiking to your stand or still-hunting.

will depend on how, when, and where you hunt. A good old-fashioned ball cap has a visor that will shield your eyes from sun and glare. You can choose from mesh back for warm weather, solid back for cool weather, insulated for extreme cold, and waterproof for when it rains or snows.

For cold you may opt for a knit cap or an insulated cap with earflaps. My first deer hunting hat was one of those Elmer Fudd jobs lined with artificial fleece. It looked pretty goofy, but it kept me warm. In extreme cold you might want the full-face protection of a balaclava, and a hooded jacket is also a nice feature to protect your head and neck from the elements.

■ You should think of your hunting clothes as a layering system, which begins with a base layer. This should be made of a quick-drying material that will wick moisture away from the body.
COURTESY OF MANUFACTURER

You have a lot more choices for the mid layer, depending on circumstances or conditions. A synthetic material, such as Trek-Lite, has better moisture-management properties for warmer conditions or when exerting yourself. If you're beating the brush, you may want heavy-duty cotton or denim, and if you're sitting in the cold, it's hard to beat fleece, which has all the insulating properties of wool and better moisture-wicking ability with less weight. It's also quiet, which is an especially important consideration for the bowhunter or still hunter. A ground hunter may also want to consider one of several other soft and silent synthetic materials with less insulation but better abrasion resistance, like Microsuede or saddle cloth. Cotton is fine for warm weather, but once wet it stays wet and saps heat from your body.

What you use for an outer layer again depends on circumstances. A fleece pullover or sweatshirt is good for milder conditions or when moving, while a down or fiberfill jacket provides more insulation when it's cold.

When it rains, you'll obviously want something waterproof, and there has been a veritable torrent of waterproof-breathable materials introduced in recent years. Most have an outer shell of tough, quiet material designed expressly for the hunter, and many are incorporated into so-called quad parkas for layering. These give you the added versatility of a waterproof outer shell and a zip-in, insulated liner jacket.

■ Hunter orange saves lives. Many states now require firearms hunters to wear an orange vest, hat, or both. With a simple pullover vest you can meet these requirements and still wear what you want underneath. Better versions have pockets for additional storage.

Another very useful piece of outerwear for the deer hunter is a vest. A simple orange vest will allow you to wear whatever you want underneath, and still meet orange-clothing requirements. An even better choice is a vest with pockets for storing shells, calls, food, and whatever else you regularly carry into the woods with you. Even with a coat and pants, it seems you can never have enough pockets. An insulated vest will also give you an extra layer when needed, without adding bulkiness to your arms.

Footwear

When you are choosing a boot for deer hunting, there are certain features that you should be looking for. First are the basics, such as support, traction, durability, and comfort. You want a boot that provides at least some ankle and arch support—greater amounts for more aggressive use or rugged terrain. Terrain may also dictate the type and amount of traction you need, more for slippery, wet, or rugged terrain, less for moderate ground. You also want a boot that will hold up. Materials like leather and Cordura nylon are good for more aggressive conditions, but you may prefer lighter material for simply walking to and from your treestand. Last, but by no means least, is comfort. That means proper support and fit and a boot that will keep your feet warm when it's cold, cool when it's hot, and dry when it's wet.

Beyond the basics, you may also want a boot that is scentproof or possibly even snakeproof. Rubber boots are generally considered the most scentproof and waterproof, but they often lack the support and durability of leather or Cordura boots. The latter, on the other hand, are not waterproof or scentproof without the addition of some sort of layering. And many, though they might stop a snake's fangs from penetrating, aren't specifically designed to do so.

So what does all this mean? For the gun hunter who likes to cover ground,

it means an ankle-high, waterproof boot with a leather and/or Cordura upper, plenty of ankle support, and a rugged sole. If it's raining or you're in wet terrain, you may want to opt for a knee-high rubber or neoprene boot, though you'll sacrifice some ankle support. High-leg boots with leather uppers and rubber bottoms, like L. L. Bean's Maine Hunting Boot, provide a good compromise, though they're not entirely waterproof.

Probably the most well-known and well-used and best all-around choice for the bowhunter is the Lacrosse Burley. This is a knee-high rubber boot with adequate ankle support for most conditions. Because it's rubber, it's also scent- and waterproof. Neoprene boots offer similar waterproof and scentproof properties with less weight but also less support.

Inside your boots you'll need socks, light for warm weather and heavy for cold. This is where that old adage: "Cotton is rotten" really applies. Even in warm weather synthetics are a better option, but they really shine in cold or wet conditions.

You can also layer your socks. Moisture-wicking sock liners are good for warm or dry conditions, but you may want a waterproof moisture-control liner like GORE-TEX for wet conditions. Over those a good wool or poly sock will add warmth and help wick away moisture.

They come in various thicknesses for varying conditions and activity levels.

Hands

Last but not least are your hands. Cold temperatures can quickly turn your bare hands into useless claws, particularly if it's wet. When it's cold and wet, you'll need something to keep your hands warm and dry. Furthermore, the bowhunter may want camo gloves to conceal the hands. Single-layer cotton is fine for moderate conditions, while fleece, wool, or insulated gloves are better when the mercury drops. When it rains or snows, GORE-TEX–lined gloves are helpful.

In any case, you want gloves that won't interfere with your shooting. Shooting gloves are a good option, as they usually have a smaller index finger for better fit into the trigger housing. My personal preference is fingerless gloves, unless it's really cold. Some gloves also come with the palms and inside the fingers lined with rubber or suede for better grip. Another option is to carry a handwarmer, which allows you to wear lighter gloves.

Scent Suppression

The whitetail's primary means of detecting danger (including the presence of humans) is its sense of smell. That's why minimizing human odors is important, particularly for the bowhunter. Specialized clothing can help in several ways. Just as you do with your regular hunting clothes, you should layer your scent-control apparel.

Begin with a moisture-wicking base layer that's been topically treated with

■ Scent control is important, particularly for bowhunters, who need to be close to their quarry.

an antimicrobial solution. These garments can be washed repeatedly with no decrease in effectiveness. In fact, the treatment usually outlasts the garment. And the moisture-wicking properties enhance effectiveness by wicking bacteria-laden moisture into the treated fabric. Over this goes a carbon-impregnated outer layer. Adopted from the military, carbon technology was first introduced to the hunting world by Scent-Lok in the early 1990s. It utilizes a layer of activated carbon—one of the most effective odor-eliminating substances known—fused to the garment's fabric. The carbon is porous, so as odor molecules pass through the material, they are trapped in the carbon pores.

Eventually, the pores fill and the suit becomes ineffective. According to Scent-Lok, you can reactivate it by heating in your dryer, which expands the holes and dislodges trapped odor molecules. However, this only restores a percentage of the fabric's odor-absorbing ability, and through repeated washing and drying, it will continue to lose its effectiveness. How much and how often you need to wash your suit will depend on several things, particularly how much odor it is exposed to. Keeping yourself clean not only reduces the chance of being detected by deer, it also increases the effectiveness, and the life span, of your Scent-Lok suit.

The very latest in odor-control technology—this time from the medical field—are ionization machines. The Moxy Scent Slayer, for example, takes stable oxygen molecules (O2) from the air and generates supercharged molecule bundles ranging as high as O14. These "predatory" molecules are lethal to all forms of bacteria, virus, mold, mildew, fungus, and other odor-causing microorganisms. Put your hunting clothes in an airtight bag, hook up the Moxy, and in 30 minutes they are virtually odor free.

The Visible Spectrum

The whitetail's next most acute sense is vision. We counteract that largely by minimizing movement and wearing camouflage clothing. Even that may not be enough, however, because deer see things we don't. Like humans, deer have two types of photoreceptors: rods and cones. In very basic terms, the rods allow us to see different shades of dark and light, and researchers have learned that the light-absorbing properties of the rods in a deer's eyes are similar to those of humans. Cones, on the other hand, are color receptors. Researchers found two classes of cones in deer, compared to three in humans. Unlike the trichromatic (three-color) vision of humans, deer vision is most sensitive to short wavelength (blue-violet) and middle-wavelength light (green-yellow). Sensitivity is lowest in the middle- to long-wavelength light (yellow-green, green, yellow, orange, and red). To them orange and red appear only as different shades of gray, which is why they aren't alarmed by blaze orange.

Of greater importance is that the whitetail's eyes lack the yellow pigment found in human eyes that acts to filter out ultraviolet light almost completely and absorbs it strongly in the violet and blue regions. As a result, a deer's sensitivity to short-wavelength light (blue and violet) is much higher than that of humans. Most conventional laundry detergents and many of the color dyes used on camouflage clothing manufactured overseas contain so-called bluing, brightening, or whitening agents. They collect light energy from a wide range of wavelengths and reradiate it in a powerful peak at a range of about 440 nanometers—near maximum sensitivity of a deer.

We don't see it because of the yellow pigment in our lenses. And in broad daylight it's probably relatively obscure to deer. But in the dim light of dawn and dusk, these brightening agents can make your clothes glow like a neon sign in the eyes of a deer.

Fortunately, there is a remedy. First, you need to determine if your camo contains brighteners by viewing it under a UV or black light to see if it glows. If it doesn't, you're in good shape, so long as you don't add any. Wash your hunting clothes only in detergents that contain no brighteners.

If your clothes glow due to dyes or fabric brighteners, there are products available, such as U-V Killer, that will permanently eliminate the effects of these additives, provided that in the future you wash your clothes only in the right detergents.

■ **Deer see the world differently from the way we humans do. If you don't take proper care of your hunting clothes, you could glow like a neon sign and never know it.** COURTESY OF MANUFACTURER

ENHANCING YOUR CAMO

Hunters killed deer long before they had camo clothes. Still, the more effective your camouflage, the less visible you will be to deer. Here are a few tips to make your camo more effective.

■ Try to wear a pattern that matches your surroundings.

■ Use different patterns on your pants and jacket to help break up your outline.

■ Don't wear old camo. Faded camo will make you appear as a light-colored blob.

■ Don't forget to camo your hands and face, and any shiny objects on your clothing or equipment that might reflect sunlight.

■ Add dimension; 3-D camo suits add another dimension of concealment to your apparel.

■ Check your camo for UV reflectance, and never wash it in conventional laundry detergent.

CHAPTER SIX

The Deer Hunter's Pack

Deer hunters are gadget junkies. While we could go afield with little more than a gun or bow, a knife, and a compass, most of us feel we *need* a lot more in order to be successful. In fact, many of the additional items we carry can be quite helpful in increasing our chances, even if they just boost our confidence. Then, of course, we need something to help us carry all that stuff. First, let's look at the contents; then we'll look at some options to tote them around in.

What you actually need can vary by circumstances. The mobile hunter will want to carry less, for obvious reasons, while the stationary hunter has more

■ Success often depends on having the right equipment, and that includes what you carry on your back.

leeway. Likewise, a quick afternoon hunt will require less gear than an all-day vigil on stand. While some items could be considered nonessential, if they can help you be more successful, why not bring them?

Compass

Tops on the list of essentials is a compass. You can use it to find your way in and out of the woods, to take a bearing on an animal's direction after the shot, and to keep track of your position while following a blood trail. It is said that you should always trust your compass, but what if you don't or it's broken? Check your other compass. A compass weighs only a few ounces, and if you ever find yourself doubting compass number one (who doesn't?), it can be very reassuring to have a second one. It could also save you from spending a night in the woods.

While they add weight and bulk to your pack, more and more hunters are using handheld GPS units. They can be invaluable when scouting or hunting. If you find a hot spot or have to leave your deer to go for help, simply mark the spot as a waypoint and your GPS will lead you right back to it. Before you enter the woods, mark your starting point so you can take the straightest route back out. The possible uses are limited only by your own imagination and inventiveness. Just remember that it is an enhancement of, not a substitute for, a compass. The batteries in your compass will never go dead.

Lights

Another essential item is a flashlight. In the morning we enter the woods before sunup, and in the afternoon we leave well after sunset. And unlike the game we pursue, humans don't see very well in the dark. A simple "mini light," of the kind that runs off two AA batteries, is all you need to find your way and keep from receiving the proverbial poke in the eye with a sharp stick. A headlamp offers an even better option because it frees up both hands—one to carry your bow or gun and one to fend off branches and cobwebs.

At the extreme end are high-tech, special-purpose lights. Some, for instance, allow you to switch between intensity and even color. Deer see poorly in the red-orange wavelengths so a red light will (theoretically) be less visible, allowing you to move about without spooking game. Low-intensity lights will similarly be less obtrusive. However, you will want a bright, high-intensity light when blood trailing, where a blue-tinted light will be more effective. As a side note, though they're bulky and not all that portable, absolutely nothing compares to a Coleman fuel lantern for nighttime blood trailing.

Cutlery

A third essential item is a knife. For field-dressing purposes, most any hunting knife will do; the key is keeping it sharp. Dull knives cause more accidents than sharp ones and make field dressing more of a chore. For this reason you may also want to carry a small steel hone or sharpener. Another handy option is a skinning hook (sometimes mistakenly referred to as a gut hook). This allows you to "zip" open the body cavity without fear of puncturing the entrails, or cutting yourself.

While it adds more weight to your pack, you may also want to have a multipurpose tool, with pliers and driver bits for field repairs, and a saw blade for limbing or boning. An alternative to the latter is a small folding saw, which can really come in handy for some last-minute trimming of shooting lanes, constructing a ground blind, or even building an overnight shelter.

Water

Yet another must is a water bottle. Even if you only intend to spend a couple of hours in the woods, you shouldn't be without water. Water will provide refreshment after a long tracking job and could save your life should you get "turned around." Under hot, dry conditions, clean water can help prevent dehydration. It can also be helpful on a cold or wet day; the biggest killer in the outdoors is hypothermia, and one of the major contributing factors is dehydration. You can also use water to clean up after field dressing or to rinse a wound.

Survival Kit

Probably one of the most overlooked items for a deer hunter's pack is a simple survival kit. Lots can happen in the woods, and you should always be prepared for the worst. A simple survival kit, weighing a few ounces, will increase your comfort and odds for survival in the case of an injury or an unintended overnight stay and could mean the difference between life and death.

Several items should be considered mandatory in your kit, including the aforementioned compass and knife. A high, shrill whistle can help rescuers find you— three short blasts is a recognized distress signal. Pieces of hard candy or an energy bar will provide sustenance and peace of mind. Whether you're in the northern forests or the southwestern desert, it can get cold at night, and you may need waterproof wooden matches and tinder for fire starting. A SPACE Brand Emergency Blanket folds up into a tiny packet yet can be used for shelter, signaling, personal protection, and warmth. Water purification tablets ensure that you will have potable water. Finally, you should have a small first-aid kit with bandages, antiseptic, and personal medication in case of injury or illness.

Optics

Another item many hunters consider essential is binoculars. I rarely go afield without them, and when I do, I invariably regret it. They are particularly important if you're still-hunting; you can stop and scan ahead with eight to ten times the visual acuity of the naked eye, making it easier to pick out a flicker of movement or a tiny part of a deer at rest. From a stand binoculars can help you spot and identify game. A patch of brown or a movement in the bushes in the distance might catch your eye, and you absolutely *never* want to use your rifle scope to view something until you're certain of what it is. (In other words, never point a gun at anything you do not intend to shoot.)

Hunting binoculars should be light (because we already tote enough other junk in the woods with us), crystal clear, and have good light-gathering ability under low-light conditions. And because we often hunt under wet conditions, they also need to be waterproof. Armor coating is also a good idea, as it will protect your binoculars from the rigors of hunting.

Binoculars in the 8x to 10x range are best for hunting. As you increase power, you generally decrease the field of view. Higher-powered binoculars are also larger. For these reasons higher power is better for the stationary hunter, lower power for the mobile hunter.

Another piece of optical equipment you might not want to do without is a range finder. This is especially true for bowhunters. One of the leading causes of missed deer is misjudged distances. Eliminate the guesswork by ranging various objects around your stand. Then when a deer appears near one, you'll know how far away he is. If time allows, you can range it and be certain.

A spotting scope may be unnecessary for the average hunter, but when hunting

■ A range finder is also an important gadget, particularly for the bowhunter.

in open range or scouting, it can be quite useful. Several compact rubber-armored versions are available specifically for the hunter. With the added magnification of 20 to 30 power, you may also want a tripod.

Miscellaneous

If you're a treestand hunter, you'll need a cord or rope to haul your bow or gun up into your stand and then something to hang it on, such as a simple screw-in hanger. You may also want a call or two, some rattling antlers or a rattling bag, your favorite scent (more on those later), and a bottle of powder or a canister of wind floaters to help you keep track of wind.

I used to think it was silly to carry a pair of rubber gloves, until I started using them. They make cleanup after field dressing a snap and could help prevent the spread of bloodborne pathogens. Though it's rare, deer can carry rabies, and though health officials claim chronic wasting disease (CWD) cannot be transmitted to humans, why take chances?

You can also wear rubber gloves when hanging any type of scent pads or canisters. A couple of large ziplock bags can be substituted for rubber gloves and be used to carry out heart and liver. They can also be used as an emergency latrine when nature calls. Last but not least, insect repellent and lip balm provide for personal comfort and protection.

Packs

Day packs come in two basic styles, fanny packs and backpacks. Within those categories are several options you can choose from, depending on your personal preference and intended use.

Fanny Packs

The smallest and simplest is the belt-type fanny pack. This is fine for short stays on stand. It's light and can be worn continuously without hindering your activity—a strong consideration if you're still-hunting. It may consist of a single, zippered pocket, though the better ones have several compartments or smaller add-on pockets to keep gear organized. The drawback is that size limits what you can carry. Moving up to a larger fanny pack offers more room and usually more pockets and interior compartments. External straps are also nice for carrying extra clothes or a jacket.

Backpacks

A standard backpack is worn with two padded shoulder straps. Better versions have smaller zippered pockets on the sides and in the back for additional storage and organization. Some also have an accessory belt,

■ Hunters have a variety of packs to choose from, depending on what and how much stuff they plan to bring into the woods on any particular day.

which is designed to stabilize the pack, not bear a load. It is not a waist belt; backpacks are meant to be worn low and secured across your hips, not on your waist.

Hybrids

If one or the other doesn't meet your needs completely, you can carry both. Or you can wear one of the hybrid back/fanny packs that have become more popular recently. They are larger, have more compartments, and have one or two shoulder straps and a rugged hip belt to help distribute the weight of a heavier pack. Whether wearing a fanny or backpack, don't overload it; this could cause discomfort or harm to your back.

Wearing and Caring

When you are wearing an unsupported fanny pack, it's important to try to distribute the load carefully and evenly and carry the weight as low on your hips as is comfortable, keeping it off the small of your back but centered on your body frame.

Most larger packs with shoulder straps come with compression straps. Don't overtighten them; they're meant to stabilize a load once it is packed, not to hold it in place. Take care of your zippers. Clean them often, and lubricate them occasionally with a silicone spray. Tape any metal zipper fobs to prevent noise should they come in contact with other metal objects. Also, keep frayed fabric trimmed back around all openings so it doesn't get caught in your zippers. Keep all buckles fastened

when not wearing the pack to prevent them from getting stepped on and broken. Inspect any stress points before each trip. Check along shoulder straps, compression straps, and the hip belt, and make any necessary repairs before going into the field by using a strong upholstery thread (or dental floss) and a heavy-duty needle.

It's also important to remember that we're talking about day packs, which are designed for one-day use. They're meant to carry extra essential items, survival gear, and possibly some food for lunch. Don't try to pack for a weekend trip. If you're staying overnight or longer, or plan on packing out your game, you'll need a much larger pack with a rigid external frame. Select the pack that is right for you, load it and wear it properly, and take care of it.

■ **A pack provides a handy way to carry all the gear you'll need for a day afield.**

CHAPTER SEVEN

Scout Now, Score Later

There is an inverse correlation between scouting time and hunting time; the more time you spend scouting, the less you'll need to spend hunting. And you shouldn't limit your scouting to the pre-season; scouting is a year-round proposition. Postseason is a great time to be in the woods because the leaves and the hunting pressure are off, and in many cases deer are still using the same areas they were in a few weeks earlier. In-season scouting is also beneficial because it tells you where the deer are and what they're doing during the time you hunt, when the pressure is on. Early spring, before leaf-out, is good, too. Not only is sign more obvious, but

■ Shed hunting is a great way to extend your season and to learn more about deer in the areas you hunt.

COURTESY OF MANUFACTURER

■ Jan Kissinger managed to collect several pairs of shed antlers and some trail cam photos from one particular buck before finally collecting the buck.

you might find shed antlers, which tells you what bucks made it through the hunting season. Still, hunters typically expend the most effort just prior to the hunting season.

Prescouting

While most of your scouting will be done in the woods, there's a lot you can do before you ever step outside the house, and it can save you considerable time when you do. Some of the most useful scouting tools a hunter can own are topographic (topo) maps and aerial photos. By combining the two you can virtually visualize your hunting area and can even scout potential stand sites right from your living room.

Maps and Photos

With a basic understanding of how to read them, topo maps can provide a tremendous amount of information. Descriptive information about both man-made and natural features appears as various colors and symbols. Forested areas appear green, while white represents open areas such as fields and croplands. The symbol for an orchard is green dots on a white background.

The juxtaposition of these details can provide important clues for locating stand sites. For instance, narrow green strips between large white areas often indicate brushy hedgerows or wooded strips in otherwise open cropland or pastures. Deer will most often travel these corridors rather than crossing open fields. Thus, they become major thoroughfares.

WHERE TO GET MAPS AND PHOTOS

- Standard 7.5' 1:25,000-scale USGS topographical maps can be obtained directly from the U.S. Geological Service (U.S. Department of the Interior, U.S. Geological Survey, 509 National Center, Reston, VA 20192) and often from a local map or sporting goods store.

- You can usually purchase aerial photos from your county Cooperative Extension offices or the Natural Resource Conservation Service (formerly Soil Conservation Service), or from the USGS.

- Computer users can get topo maps on CD-ROM from DeLorme, PO Box 298, Yarmouth, ME 04096, (207) 846-7000, www.delorme.com, or MyTopo/Maptech, 1 South Broadway, Billings, MT 59101, (877) 587-9004, www.maptech.mytopo.com. You can also view topo maps and aerial photos online at www.terraserver.com and USGS.gov.

- DeLorme's PN 20 and PN40 GPS units are also interactive with their Topo USA software, which allows you to download topo maps and aerial photos from the Internet and load them into the GPS unit.

■ A handheld GPS unit has so many uses for scouting. You can log in locations from your maps and find them easily. And if you find a hot spot in the field, you can store it as a waypoint and find your way back to it.

Such areas may be especially productive if they connect two or more larger blocks of woods. Often, you'll find these strips occur along the riparian area or the floodplain of rivers, streams, and brooks, which are traditionally good spots for stand placement.

Because they usually occur along property lines, the boundaries between fields and forest are often straight with square corners, and deer movement will be funneled around these corners. Just as the outside corner of a field will funnel deer movement around it, an inside corner will funnel deer into it. In the late season

this is especially true if the field contains a carbohydrate-rich crop, such as soybeans or corn. Deer will use dense cover as much as possible to reach an open area, and an inside corner provides a little extra bit of cover before they come into the open. It also acts like a funnel, with the spout right at the corner.

Water appears as blue on the map—blue tint for water bodies and large waterways and blue lines for streams. While smaller streams and their riparian corridors indicate good travel areas, larger waterways and water bodies represent obstacles to deer movement. They're most likely to cross at narrow points along a wide river, and movement will be concentrated around the top and bottom ends of lakes and ponds. And in drier regions water bodies and wetlands are deer magnets.

Swamps, bogs, and marshes are indicated by a blue wetland symbol; wetland symbols on a green tint indicate a swamp, while wetland symbols on a white background indicate a marshy area. The biggest, thickest, nastiest swamps are where you'll find those sagacious old bucks hiding out.

Even better, if you can find topographical islands, small areas of higher ground, in the swamp, you can bet there will be deer beds there. If you don't care to brave these quagmires, look for nearby feeding areas (orchards, fields), or wooded strips where you may catch the deer coming to or from bedding.

Another useful map feature, especially in hilly terrain, is contour lines. These brown lines represent points of equal elevation. Parallel contour lines appear at 10-foot intervals, which means each line represents a 10-foot change in elevation. The distance between adjacent lines is called the contour interval. The closer the lines are together, the steeper the contour or grade. On a steep grade, lines will be very close together, while in relatively flat areas lines will be some distance apart.

Study the contour intervals on your map, and you can begin to visualize what the terrain looks like and where the deer are more likely to move through it. They usually take the path of least resistance. Steep ridges will funnel deer movement into narrow areas. Saddles or low areas between peaks are great spots to place a stand. On bigger ridges or mountains you'll sometimes see wide, flat areas, or benches, along the side slope. Whitetails love to travel and bed on these benches.

Anyone who has hunted steep terrain knows most of the deer trails run more or less parallel to the ridges or angle up and down gradually. More often than not, the deer will feed or move along a side slope, round the point, then move back along the other side rather than hoofing it up and over. The same is true at the head of steep draws.

Combining aspect and slope from maps with cover types from photos can also help you hone down your list of possible stand locations. In colder regions, particularly later in the season, deer will more likely be on the sunny side of slopes—east in the morning and west in the evening. Also, late in the season and during midday periods, deer will more likely be in the densest cover, the bottoms of draws and hollows or along waterway margins.

Topo maps also contain a number of man-made features that are useful in finding your way to and from potential stand sites. Jeep or foot trails are represented by a single dashed line; unimproved or dirt roads by parallel dashed lines; and light-duty, hard-surface, or improved roads by solid parallel lines.

Hunters should also be able to recognize transmission lines or gas line rights-of-way, which appear as single or multiple dotted and dashed lines for the former and narrow white strips for the latter. Where permissible, power lines provide an easy access route to backwoods areas, either by foot or by vehicle. Some hunters also like to set up on the edges of power lines. Power line rights-of-way must be maintained. Cutting and other forms of vegetation suppression result in an abundance of grasses, forbs, woody shoots, and other preferred deer foods.

Reading Signs

Much of your scouting will still be done on the ground, and there's a lot you can learn from the various signs you'll encounter.

Tracks

Probably the most abundant and obvious sign you'll find will be tracks and trails, and being able to interpret them is important to your success. Deer have a cloven hoof that makes a heart-shaped impression, and the bigger the track, the bigger the deer. Track size varies on a geographical gradient, but in general, a track approximately 2 inches long was made by a yearling, a track of 3 inches or more is an adult deer, and one much over 3.5 to 4 inches is a mature deer and quite likely a buck. Similarly, a narrow track with sharp edges is more likely a younger deer, while a broader, rounded track is an older deer.

There has been much disagreement over whether it's possible to differentiate a buck's track from a doe's. The only certain way is to see the deer that made it. However, there are some guidelines that can help you differentiate with some degree of confidence.

One way is by looking at size. Once a deer reaches maturity, its hoof may not grow much longer, but it will grow wider. If you find a 4-inch track that's nearly as wide as it is long, you're almost certainly following a mature buck.

Another way to determine gender is by track placement. Like most mammals, male and female deer are built differently. Females have broad hips and narrow shoulders, while the opposite is true for bucks. In both cases, the front foot is smaller than the rear. As a deer walks it will put its rear foot down on top of, or very close to, where the front foot stepped. In the case of a buck, the smaller, rear track will be slightly inside the larger front track. With a doe the rear track will be slightly outside the front track.

Buck and doe tracks can also sometimes be differentiated by other characteristics. Bucks, especially during and after the rut, will drag their feet when they walk, so prominent drag marks may indicate a buck. Due to their heavier weight, buck tracks may also appear more splayed, turned outward and wider apart. A heavier deer will also sink deeper into snow or soft ground.

In snow you can also use urine marks as an indicator. Does will urinate in their tracks with a wide, irregular spray. A buck's urine is usually more of a direct stream, and they may also leave dribble marks as they walk.

How the deer is traveling is also important. Short strides and meandering tracks indicate feeding, while straight, deliberate tracks indicate the deer are traveling through the area on their way to somewhere else.

Trails

Trails are another thing to look for while scouting. Finding a heavily trodden trail is exciting, and the temptation is strong to set up on it immediately. But before you do you should try to determine why, when, and how often the trail is being used and by which animals.

■ You can learn a lot from tracks, such as the size of the deer that made them and which way it was headed. If you're consistently finding big tracks in a particular location, your search may be over. COURTESY OF MANUFACTURER

A simple, well-beaten path, sometimes called a runway, indicates a defined corridor that deer use on a regular basis. It might be a runway between bedding and feeding areas or approaching a field edge. If you find one, look at the tracks in it. Do they point in one direction, indicating one-way travel, or are the deer traveling in both directions?

Also, consider the trail in relation to surrounding cover, habitat, and wind direction. If the tracks are approaching a bedding area, that might be a better morning stand. Conversely, if they head toward a feeding area, you may opt for an afternoon hunt. Deer will often approach a field from the downwind side and leave it on the upwind side.

You should also look at the size of the tracks, if possible. Does and fawns are much more prone to following trails. Bucks, especially mature bucks, tend to avoid heavy trails, instead sticking to thicker cover and paralleling the heavier trail from the downwind side. This is important, especially for the bowhunter, if you're looking to set up on an older buck.

Droppings

Deer droppings can be of some utility in scouting, if you know how to interpret what you see. It's difficult, if not impossible to determine the sex of the deer that made them, but they can at least tell you there are deer in the area. And on hard, trackless ground they provide an alternate indication of deer use. Soft, moist, green pellets indicate fresh droppings, while harder, darker-colored pellets are older. Deer that have been feeding on herbaceous vegetation or soft mast such as apples may leave loose clumped droppings. Later in the fall, when their diet switches to browse and hard mast, their droppings will be more pelletlike and fibrous.

Deer that are moving about, traveling, or feeding will typically drop a scattering of pellets. If you find a clumped mass, that's a good indication that the deer may have bedded nearby.

■ An accumulation of fresh droppings is a good indication deer have been feeding in the area recently.

■ Acorns of the white oak are sweeter, and deer prefer them over red oak acorns, while they last.

Feeding

Find the food source, and you'll find the deer. This is especially true later in the season as food becomes scarce. Evidence of feeding can be a particularly valuable type of sign, especially if it's fresh and concentrated. Deer will paw up leaves as they search for acorns, much like turkeys do. But their scratchings will be more random and less well defined than those of turkeys, which often appear as larger, V-shaped patches of bare ground.

You should also look at the vegetation. Deer lack upper incisors. When they nip a twig off, it will appear more ragged and torn. Rabbits, on the other hand, will make a neat clip when they browse. If you observe this type of browsing sign, pay particular attention to the type of plants deer are feeding on, then try to find concentrations of those species.

Beds

The advantage of finding deer beds is obvious; they tell you where deer are spending the vast majority of their time. In general, deer beds close to a food source or in more open areas are probably night beds. You'll more often find day beds in the densest and most difficult-to-access cover but not always. Deer have the miraculous ability to hide in plain sight and may bed in some quite obvious but often overlooked areas. I once found a group of deer beds in a small patch of cover that I drove by every day on the way to my stand.

Unless there's snow, beds may be difficult to find, as they consist of little more than a shallow depression or a patch of flattened leaves or grass. They generally range from 25 to 40 inches long, with doe-fawn and doe beds being on the smaller end—roughly 35 inches or less. Another

■ Deer spend most of their day bedded, so knowing where they bed can be particularly important to your success.

hint for sexing beds is the number. A doe will bed with her offspring and possibly other does. A buck, on the other hand, will be more inclined to bed alone. If you find a medium and a large bed together during the rut, there's a good possibility it is a buck tending a doe.

Rubs and Scrapes

Rubs and rub lines are among the most misunderstood and misinterpreted types of deer sign you'll find. When you find them, about the only thing you can be certain of is that they were made by a buck. A single rub, in and of itself, is of little use unless you can place it in some perspective of space and time. There are also different kinds of rubs and scrapes.

Rubs

You'll recall from chapter 1 that, sometime in late August or early September, shortening daylight triggers an increase in testosterone in bucks. Circulation to the antlers is cut off; velvet dies, and the bucks begin to rub. Bucks are fairly sedentary at this time of year, sticking close to a core area and often associating with other bucks in bachelor groups. If you find fresh rubs very early in the season, it's a good indication there is at least one buck, perhaps more, using the area.

However, bucks will soon shift into fall mode, traveling more and over a wider area. They'll still remain fairly routine until the rut, however. This is a good time to look for and hunt rub lines.

■ Small rubs could be made by any buck, but in general, big rubs mean big bucks.

Like scrapes, deer will often use the same rubs in successive years. In fact, rubbing on specific trees has been documented in excess of the life span of a single deer. Like scrapes, traditional rubs are usually located along well-traveled trails, where many deer will encounter them, and they serve as a sort of visual and olfactory message board.

The territorial rubs of a mature buck generally occur in a consistent pattern. They're typically on single trees, often spaced some distance apart, and usually in a line. A line of regularly rubbed trees is a good indication you're in an area used routinely by at least one buck.

The size of the rubbed trees *may* be an important indicator of the size of the buck.

Rubs on small trees don't necessarily mean small bucks, but only big bucks rub big trees. Larger bucks also tend to rub higher on tree trunks.

Rub lines, like trails, will also indicate direction of travel. As you follow the rub line, note which side of the tree is rubbed. Is the line heading toward feeding or bedding cover? Determining this can help you decide when it is best to hunt.

Some rubs can be deceiving. An acquaintance of mine once related a story of how he had found what he called a buck's "core area." He described a patch of wrist-thick alders, all of which had been stripped of bark from knee to chest height. He hunted there for a week and never caught so much as a glimpse of the buck that made them. He could have saved himself a lot of wasted time if he had understood what he was looking at.

Those prerut sparring matches, designed to sort out the pecking order, are often preceded by a lot of posing and parading. If this fails to intimidate, rival bucks may take out their aggression on the local foliage. This is usually the cause of fresh multistemmed rubs. These rubs occur at random locations where the two bucks happened to cross paths and mean little in terms of core areas or hideouts.

Rubs on or along field edges are also mighty tempting to the neophyte hunter. But studies have shown that most rubbing occurs at night, and this is especially true of open areas, such as field edges. However, you may be able to follow a rub line back into the woods a ways and locate a staging area, where deer mill about during those critical last minutes of daylight.

Scrapes

Scrapes are like an olfactory dating service for whitetails. They're created when a buck paws away the surface duff and urinates on the exposed earth to advertise his presence and dominance to other bucks in the area and his interest and availability to the local female contingent. In areas with a balanced buck-to-doe ratio and light hunting pressure, the dominant buck in an area does most of the scraping. Other local bucks may do some scraping but usually limit their activity around traditional breeding scrapes to scent-marking the overhanging licking branch.

■ Trail cameras are an unobtrusive and labor-saving way to scout your hunting area. And knowing there's a big deer in the area you hunt can be a real confidence booster.

■ **Though most scraping is done at night, bucks may scent-check scrapes during the day, particularly just prior to does coming into heat.** COURTESY OF MANUFACTURER

Timing is key to understanding and hunting scrapes. Scrape initiation typically begins sometime around the first full moon after the autumnal equinox. However, after opening his scrape line, a buck may "lay off" for several days. Furthermore, many of those early scrapes will

never be revisited; they may have been the result of a buck blowing off a little prerut angst.

As the breeding period nears, however, bucks will begin visiting scrapes on a more regular basis. This is why you may need to make successive scouting trips to see which scrapes are being tended. Also, you only have a fairly narrow window of opportunity to catch a buck on or near his scrape. Once the first does begin coming into estrus, bucks will abandon scrapes for several weeks.

There are several important things to keep in mind with regard to scrapes. First, they are scent posts. The buck's already uncanny sense of smell is on full alert when he's scent-checking a scrape, so you've got to keep your odor at an absolute minimum around them. Also, a buck will often approach a scrape and scent-check it from some distance downwind and may not actually go all the way to it. Finally, most scrapes are made under cover of darkness. Still, I have observed bucks making scrapes during daylight and even taken a couple that were in the process.

Scouting can play a vital role in your success. Knowing where the deer are before you hunt can save lots of time and frustration. It's also a great excuse to get out in the woods and get a little fresh air and exercise and learn more about the creatures you pursue.

CHAPTER EIGHT

Take a Stand

The concept of hunting from an elevated perch isn't new, though the perches themselves have changed dramatically over the last two decades. Treestand hunting can sometimes be a slow, boring method, requiring a lot of patience. However, it can be a significantly more effective and successful technique for taking deer, offering several major advantages. Of course, there are some disadvantages, too.

Advantages

Visibility

Michigan's treestand regulations provide an insightful description of one of the major advantages of using a treestand. The regulations define a raised platform as "a horizontal surface constructed or manufactured by a person that increases the field of vision of a person using the horizontal surface beyond the field of vision

■ From an elevated position, you can see deer approaching from a long way off. You can also move more without being detected, and your scent is carried farther away.

that would normally be attained by that person standing on the ground."

Once you're 10 or 12 feet above the ground, it's amazing how much better your visibility is. Suddenly, you can see over obstacles that impaired your visibility on the ground, such as brush, limbs, deadfalls, even small knolls. You can see approaching game from a much greater distance, reducing the chances of being taken by surprise. You can also see other hunters better, and presumably, you'll be more visible to them, reducing the chances of an accident.

This edge can be used to your advantage in a number of ways. Deer learn very quickly where they are safe, and they'll head for the thickets when the pressure is on. A treestand allows you to hunt over thick cover where ground hunting would be impossible. You'll also realize an advantage in uneven topography.

Movement

Another advantage is related to movement. Sitting on the ground, you have to be much more careful about movement. Simple things like scratching your ear, taking a bite of a sandwich, or shifting around to make yourself comfortable could all give you away. This is especially true on windy or wet days, when the sound of an approaching deer is masked, and it may see you before you're aware of its presence.

You can get away with a lot more movement from an elevated platform than you can on the ground, which is helpful

should you have to move to prepare for a shot. This is especially critical for bowhunters, who must draw on a deer when it is at extremely close range, but it also applies to gun hunters.

Scent

Yet another advantage, particularly for bowhunters, is scent. Deer rely on their sense of smell even more than on their eyesight, and getting up above the ground significantly reduces your chances of being detected. Just the same, you need to be careful and always pay attention to wind direction, just as you would when hunting from the ground.

Disadvantages

Mobility

There are some disadvantages to elevated stands, one of the most obvious being mobility. Once you build or hang your stand, you're committed to that spot, at least for the short term. Portable stands are a better option, as they allow you the flexibility to change positions later if needed. Furthermore, deer quickly learn where danger lies, and once a permanent stand is detected, its usefulness becomes limited. Also, movement patterns may change from year to year.

Labor

Treestand hunting also means more work and possibly an extra trip into the woods. You may choose to hang your stand in advance or bring it with you when you hunt. Either way, it's more gear to lug in and more commotion in your hunting area. When possible, it's often better to hang your stand in advance of your hunt, and this is best done during the middle of the day, when deer movement is at a minimum (though you should never rule out hanging a stand in the middle of the night if necessary). The key, in any case, is to do plenty of advance scouting before you hang your stand.

Stand Locations

So where should you hang your stand? To a great extent, that will depend on when, where, and how you hunt. Your first and most important consideration will be wind direction. You want to be downwind of where you think the deer will be moving. However, don't set all of your stands according to prevailing wind patterns. Set one or two for bad weather, when wind directions are usually from a nontypical direction.

Obviously, you'll want to set your stand where you think the deer will be, and if you've done your scouting properly, you've already narrowed down the search considerably. Now you just need to refine it.

Deer habitat can be broken down into three general types: feeding, bedding, and transition or travel areas. Bedding areas are best left alone, except in extreme circumstances. Still, it's helpful to know where they are. In most cases you'll be

hunting either feeding areas or travel corridors between bedding and feeding.

This is a gross generality, but daylight deer movement tends to be better in the afternoon than in the morning. Furthermore, you can move into your afternoon stand in daylight, before deer become active. For these reasons, it's more effective to hunt afternoon stands in or near feeding areas.

In the morning deer are already up and moving, and you have to find your way

■ **Paying attention to wind direction is critical to stand placement. Try to place your stands downwind of trails, and set a few stands for nontypical wind directions.** COURTESY OF MANUFACTURER

in the dark. At this time of day, you may be better off hunting closer to bedding areas. In heavily hunted areas especially, deer will be leaving feeding areas and heading back to bed early, and you may only have a short window of opportunity to intercept them. You can extend that window by setting up closer to bedding. Furthermore, if you get in early enough, it's less likely they will be there ahead of you.

In either case, you can play it safe by hunting transition areas. This includes both travel areas and places where deer stage before feeding. Travel areas are also great places to hunt during the rut, when bucks may be cruising at any time of the day. Then, you should hunt as close to bedding areas as you can get without spooking deer. Rutting bucks will often move from one bedding area to the next during mid-day periods searching for hot does.

You still need to decide where, in these three habitat types, you'll place your stand.

Again, that will depend on local circumstances, but there are some generalities that can help you. Perhaps the best general rule is to look for funnels—any feature, natural or man-made, that concentrates deer movement into a narrow area. Incidentally, all of this advice also applies to stump sitters as well.

Funnels come in many forms, and once you learn to recognize them, it will open up a whole new world of successful hunting for you. While deer can, and will, overcome most obstacles, they'll most often take the path of least resistance. They also tend to avoid open areas. A gap in a stone wall or a wire fence, a narrow strip of woods between fields, a saddle between two peaks, even a strip of denser cover are all funnels and are great places to hang a stand. Locate a funnel that connects feeding and bedding areas, and you've got two elements working for you.

Water

Water creates some of the best funnels in the deer woods. Deer are excellent swimmers but tend to avoid water crossings, especially in larger waterways or water bodies. In the Midwest and West, waterways provide the only dense cover and thus act as funnels. They also represent obstacles. You'll often find that most of the trails near a river run parallel to it rather than across it. And the crossings will be where the river narrows or is shallow. The outside bend in a river, the bottom or top of a lake, or just below a beaver dam make great funnels. The best ones are where deer can't exploit prevailing winds to sense danger ahead.

Topography

Topography also creates funnels. Deer, like people, tend to avoid steep areas. Rather than cross a steep ridge, they'll often travel parallel to it, crossing around the point or at the head—and these are great corners to set up on. Setting up high on such corners offers several advantages. First, most of the action will be below you so you can concentrate on one direction.

■ **Topography creates deer funnels, and by studying topographic maps you can plot where to place your stands.** COURTESY OF MANUFACTURER

Man-Made Funnels

While it does destroy open space, development can have some beneficial side effects for the hunter. Narrow strips of woods between houses suddenly become deer funnels. Even in more rural agricultural areas, fences provide ideal barriers to deer movement. Deer can jump fences as high as 10 feet, but a 3-foot-high fence usually provides enough of a barrier to coax them alongside it. Even the gap in a stone wall will show much heavier use by deer than other areas along the wall's length. The higher and wider the wall, the better it functions as a funnel.

The timber industry is responsible for creating some fantastic man-made habitat funnels. Narrow wooded strips between clear-cuts function in the same manner as those between open agricultural fields. Furthermore, these strips are often along watercourses, where natural cover is densest and contains plenty of food. Many of these areas were probably traditional travel routes even before adjacent land was cut, and deer will feed casually through them.

Food Plots

Stand placement is an important element to hunting food plots. Establishing food plots is a labor-intensive proposition and therefore usually a long-term commitment. Because of that, you may be inclined to put up permanent stands, which is a good idea for gun hunters but a bad idea for bowhunters. Deer quickly learn the

Second, being higher up offers the same advantages as being in a treestand: greater visibility and less chance of being scented. Third, it's easier to move down than up.

As previously mentioned, saddles or low areas between peaks are also great spots to place a stand because they provide an easier route for deer. On bigger ridges or mountains, you'll sometimes see wide, flat areas, or benches, along the side slopes. Whitetails love to travel and bed on these benches, and you'll often see side slope trails funneling through them.

location of permanent stands and how to avoid them. That avoidance may only be a dozen yards or so, but it could be enough to take them out of bow range.

Leave yourself plenty of options. Rather than one stand tree, pick out two or three in close proximity. And you don't necessarily have to hunt overlooking the plot either. Stands just inside the woods can also be productive, especially during the rut, when bucks may be scent-checking doe groups from downwind of the plot. When you are hunting the plot, leave yourself plenty of cover in front. Deer are especially jittery when in the open and more likely to pick you out.

Light direction may be almost as important as wind direction when hunting food plots. There will only be shade along one side; the other will be in direct sunlight. If at all possible, try to set stands so you'll be in the shade, with the sun at your back. That means your morning stands should face west and your evening stands east, if the wind allows. This will give you an edge.

Some Final Thoughts

The type of stand you use may determine where you should hunt and vice versa. For example, food plots will be a reliable, long-term food source and a good place for a permanent or semipermanent stand, such as a tower or ladder. Natural food sources can vary from year to year and even within the hunting season. Red oaks typically produce nuts in alternate years, and white oak acorns are often gone before the end

■ Stands overlooking feeding areas are often best hunted in the afternoon as you can get into them in daylight, well in advance of feeding times, without spooking deer.

of the season. Here you might prefer a portable stand that you can move in reaction to seasonal or annual food availability.

One of the most important pieces of advice I can offer is this: Don't overhunt your stand. Your best chance will probably come the first time on stand—assuming you've done your scouting homework. The more you visit it, the more you'll disturb the area and leave scent. It won't take deer long to pattern your movements, discover your stand, and avoid it.

This is why it's helpful to have multiple stands. I rarely hunt the same stand on consecutive days or more than two or three times a week. It's tempting to hunt one stand repeatedly, especially when the sign is smoking hot, but if you don't connect right away, you could end up burning out a very good location.

Try to approach your stand from a downwind direction and one that will cause the least disturbance. A water approach is ideal. Also, if you approach during daylight, stalk the last 100 yards or so. The reason you put your stand in a particular location is that deer use it, and there's a very good possibility they'll be there when you arrive. On numerous occasions I've jumped bedded deer very close to my stands.

Safety

Any discussion on treestands must include some mention of safety. Injuries related to treestands are the number-one cause of

■ **Don't overhunt your stand. Every time you visit the woods, you leave scent behind, and it won't take deer long to figure out how to avoid you.**

hunting accidents. In one respect a treestand is like a gun. When used properly and safely, it is little more than a tool. When used improperly, it can become a dangerous weapon. Read and follow the safety instructions that come with your stand carefully. Never lower or raise a loaded weapon from your stand. And always, always, always wear a safety harness when in your stand. It's a minimal investment that could one day save your life.

CHAPTER NINE

Food Plots: If You Build Them, They Will Come

It used to be that most hunters were content to hunt the land that was available to them, seeking out better deer habitat where it occurred and leaving habitat

■ Like scents and calls, food plots are just another tool designed to attract deer.

management to state and federal agencies. Many still are, but a good deal more attention nowadays is being directed toward managing private land for deer. And while earlier efforts were largely undertaken by leaseholders and large commercial landowners, more and more individuals with smaller holdings, some as small as 100 acres, are getting into the action.

There are some obvious advantages to building food plots. Improving the quality of the habitat improves the quality of the deer on your land. It also allows your land to support more deer. And managing land for deer also improves habitat for other species, such as upland game and turkeys. Finally, food plots can also help improve your success rate.

Food plots can be divided into two general categories: hunting and feeding. Feeding plots are intended to keep the deer on your property healthy and present year-round and are generally larger and laid out for agricultural efficiency. Hunting plots are intended to attract deer in the fall and to offer shot opportunities. They're often smaller and more irregular in shape. We'll go into more detail below.

Plan before you plant. Make sure you do your homework first. Otherwise all your efforts in the field could be wasted. COURTESY OF MANUFACTURER

Proper Planning

The first step in establishing food plots is to gather baseline data; look at what you have for a starting point and honestly evaluate how far you can or want to go. Existing conditions, acreage, topography, and surrounding land uses should all be factored in. Obviously, it's much easier to build your plots in a field than in a forest, if you can. It's also generally true that your plots will be more effective if you can place them where deer are already inclined to travel.

The key to all food plots is soil. Areas with the best soils will produce the best crops with the least effort. To find out where the best soils exist, you can consult your county agent or a soil survey. There is a soil survey available for virtually

every county in the country. These books, available from your local USDA Natural Resource Conservation Service (NRCS) office, contain soil maps and descriptions of the soil types, including physical properties and arability.

However, you may not always be able to exploit the best soils. Your soil might be deficient, or you may want to strategically position your plots in areas of poorer soils. In either case, you can increase soil quality with mineral fertilizer, but you need to know how much and what kind to use.

The most important step in establishing food plots is to test the soil's properties, and one of the most important is pH. This simple step could save you thousands of otherwise wasted dollars and hours.

CUTOVERS: THE OTHER FOOD PLOT

One of the biggest drawbacks to building food plots is the cost, in terms of both time and money. However, simply by cutting a forested area, you are, in effect, creating a food plot. Increased sunlight means more growth, and many of the early successional plant species that sprout are preferred by deer. Proceeds from timber sales can also be put toward more intensive food-plot construction. Keep in mind, however, that you'll receive the greatest long-term benefits by using a cutting plan prepared by a licensed forester.

Test kits are available from your county agent, local USDA NRCS office, university extension, or several commercial seed companies. Be sure to include a description of your intended use, as many test results will come with recommendations on how best to treat your soils for that use. The biggest problem is typically acidic soils, which can be cured with lime. Nitrogen and phosphorus will also help improve the growth and palatability of plants.

As mentioned earlier, soil quality is only one consideration when locating your plots and is often more important with feeding plots. Other factors may be just as important, especially when positioning hunting plots. If possible, you should study the wind, weather, and thermal patterns and existing deer travel patterns on your hunting area the season before you lay out your food plots.

A couple of very useful tools for this step include a topo map and an aerial photo. You may recall from chapter 7 how topography and habitat influence deer movement. The more you can work with existing conditions, the easier to build and more effective your plots will be. To some extent they may also help you predict wind and thermal patterns, which can help you save time if you don't want to burn a season checking wind.

You also need to put your plot plan into perspective. Consider how you'll approach the plots; you want a good, downwind access. Look at their juxtaposition with surrounding habitat types. The closer to dense bedding cover your plot is, the longer its effective hunting duration. A small plot in the middle of the woods may be more effective than one near a large clover field, though that's not always the case.

If you can, lay out both hunting and feeding plots strategically. Larger feeding plots provide enough of the right types of food to keep deer on your property year round, so they're less likely to wander onto the neighbor's grounds. But because of their size, deer will use them mostly at night. The smaller hunting plots then act as staging areas and are best located between bedding and nighttime feeding areas. That means deer are more apt to use them during twilight. If there are good feeding areas on or near your hunting grounds, you may be able to reduce your effort by establishing smaller hunting plots nearby. Also try to put hunting plots on major travel routes and adjacent to traditional rub lines.

Size Matters

There are several reasons that smaller is better for hunting plots. First and foremost, deer feel more secure in a smaller opening during daylight hours than they do in a larger one. Second, they'll be more likely to stick close to the edge, in bow or gun range, in a smaller plot, while the exact opposite is often true of larger food plots—they often head right for the middle. Similarly, more of your plot will be inside your effective range.

There are a few drawbacks to smaller plots that the hunter should be aware of. One: Deer tend not to linger in them long. Two: If they're surrounded by dense security cover, as they should be, you may not

EXCLOSURES

Exclosures can help you determine how much use your food plot is getting. It can sometimes be difficult to evaluate how much the deer are using your plots and which plants they prefer. One solution is to build an exclosure or utilization cage. Simply make a round cage from 12 feet of 3-foot-high welded wire and attach it to a wooden stake. You can easily see the difference between plants in your plot and those inside the cage, where the deer cannot reach.

see the deer until they are in range. That means you've got to be on full alert, all the time.

Shape

Shape is another consideration. Again, hunting plots should be set up for close encounters with game. Long and narrow is a good configuration, especially for bowhunting. This allows you to increase the area of your plot, while still keeping most of it effectively within range. You may even be able to set up several stands on the same plot, for hunting different wind directions.

Irregular shapes also allow you to plan multiple ambush sites and potentially funnel deer in a particular direction or to a particular location. Once in the open, deer tend to follow the long axis of a relatively linear plot. If your plot is hourglass shaped, the narrow middle makes for an ideal stand location. They'll also follow the edges, so an outside corner, where natural cover juts out into the plot, is another good stand location.

Bowhunters especially may want to consider hanging some stands back away from the plot edge. Older bucks may stage in areas 30 to 50 yards back into the cover, where they'll scent-check the plot before venturing into it. Set your stands on the downwind side of an approach trail. You may not see as many deer, but you might see bigger ones.

Setting up back in the woods is also a better tactic for morning hunts. You won't empty the field when you go in to your stand, and you can catch deer as they filter out to bedding areas.

Creating Cover

You can also use natural and man-made cover around your plots to make deer go where you want them to. Slash leftover from cutting makes a great natural barrier. If you use heavy equipment to build your plots, you can also push stumps, roots, and brush into windrows to build a barrier. You can also use these windrows and brush tangles as a ground blind. It's important to keep wind direction in mind as you build them. Your object is to keep deer from approaching your stand location from downwind.

■ **Brush cleared from food plots can be used to direct deer around your plot and make them go where you want them to.**

You should also bear in mind that deer movement around food plots may not be the same as in the woods. In the woods they rely more on their nose than their eyes. When approaching an open area, they can utilize both by approaching from upwind because they can see what's in front of them and smell what's behind them. So don't expect them to always approach from downwind. Bucks especially may initially approach from a downwind direction, then circle around to the upwind side before stepping into the open. This is where your windrows come in. The more difficult you make it for them, the less likely they'll sneak in behind you.

You can also use slash and treetops left over from plot construction to create dense security cover. Initially, they'll act as a barrier, protecting young vegetation from the hungry deer. Because the deer can't reach it, more vegetation can grow in the tangles. Eventually, the dead wood deteriorates, and you're left with a dense travel corridor.

Feed 'Em Right

Another obviously important consideration for your food plots is what you plant in them, and that will depend, to some extent, on their purpose. You may recall from chapter 1 that the whitetail's diet shifts throughout the year. You want your feeding plots to provide year-round nutrition, while hunting plots should be planted primarily for fall utilization.

■ Make sure you plant a blend rather than mono-culture seed. The different plant varieties will have different growth rates, maturation dates, and palatability peaks, meaning there will always be something for deer to eat.

Your best option is to pick a blend of the big three food-plot plants: clover, chicory, and brassicas. This high-protein forage will meet the nutritional needs of lactating does and their fawns and help put inches on your bucks' antlers. For hunting plots you may want a blend that also has high-carbohydrate foods, such as wheat and oats, which will further help deer put on the pounds and make it through the winter.

In any case, blends or mixtures are always better than pure-strain seeds. They're sort of a salad bar for deer. The different plant varieties will have different growth rates, maturation dates, and palatability peaks, meaning there will always

PERENNIALS VS. ANNUALS

■ Brassicas become more important later in the fall. They tend to be bitter tasting until the first frosts. Then the starches change to sugars, and deer relish them.

There are two general categories of food-plot plants, and each has its pros and cons. Annuals must be planted every year—annually. This means more cost and more labor. However, they tend to produce higher yields. Perennials will persist for several years but are not as productive. Because most of the fall foods tend to be annuals, they are a better choice for hunting plots, while perennial blends are a better option for year-round feeding plots.

be something for deer to eat. They'll also respond differently to various weather conditions. Under warm, dry conditions, clover goes dormant because of stress. Chicory, however, has a deep taproot and is still vibrant and drought tolerant. Chicory blends may be more expensive, but they are well worth the extra few dollars if you want to keep your deer well fed throughout seasonal and climatological changes.

You might be tempted to save a few dollars by going down to the local co-op to buy your seed. Don't. You want a blend that has been engineered for food plots. Your local blends are more likely to contain predominantly red clover and alfalfa, which make great cattle forage but tend to have more coarse fiber and thus are less digestible to deer. Most wildlife seed companies have done extensive research on which blends are most palatable to deer. You just need to determine your intended use and select the recommended blend; there are dozens to choose from.

Don't be afraid to try different blends, either. You may find that one type or brand performs better on your property or that your deer prefer one type over another. Some wildlife seed companies will even recommend different blends for different regions or climate zones.

Planting

Once you've done all the preliminary work, the actual planting is a fairly straightforward process, albeit labor intensive. If the area is already vegetated, you'll first need to remove existing vegetation. This can be done mechanically, chemically, or through a combination of both. Treat the area with an herbicide such as Round-Up or Arsenal, and let it stand for about a week.

Next, turn the soil with a disk or plow. This will turn dead organic matter into the soil and break up clods. Then compact the soil with a roller to remove air pockets and provide a firmer seed bed for better germination.

Now you can broadcast your seed. Be sure to follow specific recommendations for the amount of seed per acre. Your inclination might be to overseed, but this will only lead to plants outcompeting one another and poorer growth. Scrimping, on the other hand, will only lead to a sparser crop.

Use some type of broadcast spreader, rather than simply hand-casting, as the latter can be wasteful. You can also broadcast fertilizer at this time. Then run over your plot with a roller or, better, a culti-packer. Moisture is crucial to germination, so your crop will be more successful if you can plant just before a rain. Now stand back, and let nature take its course.

Conclusion

Food plots are a great way to increase your odds for success. Your land will attract more and healthier deer and concentrate them into more defined areas. In addition, working the land to produce a crop, in this case deer, will make your success all the more rewarding when it finally comes.

■ Before planting it's a good idea to eliminate existing vegetation that will compete with food-plot species for nutrients and space.

■ Working the land to produce a crop will make your success feel all the more rewarding, when it finally comes.

CHAPTER TEN

Calling All Deer

Many novice hunters, and a few veterans, are surprised to learn that deer are actually quite vocal. We just seldom hear them, partly because most of their vocalizations are very soft and quiet (an important point to keep in mind) and because they don't call as frequently as other species; for instance, elk or turkeys. Still, deer have a diverse repertoire of calls, each with a different meaning. Being able to speak fluent whitetail means knowing how and when to imitate these calls, which can add a very valuable weapon to their arsenal for success.

It's important to remember, however, that calling is not a panacea. Just like scents and lures, calling will not make you a better hunter or make up for your inadequacies. Deer calls work, sometimes. Reactions I've witnessed to deer calling range from nonchalant indifference to flat-out fleeing. However, when done properly, at the right time and under the right conditions, calling can be very effective.

Deer calls and calling can be divided into two general categories: vocalizations and rattling. Vocalizations, in turn, can be grouped into categories based on the season or the behavior, sex, or age of the deer making them.

■ Calling won't work all the time, but when done correctly and under the right circumstances, it can sometimes tip the balance in your favor. COURTESY OF MANUFACTURER

Vocalizations

The most common method of calling deer is by imitating one or more of the many vocalizations they use to communicate with one another. Each has different meaning. Deer calling also has a certain seasonality to it. While some calls will work well throughout the hunting season, many work best only during certain periods of the deer's annual behavioral cycle. This is where some of what you learned in chapter 1 comes into the equation.

Fawn Calls

Fawn calls are most effective early in the fall. A doe's maternal instinct is still very strong, and the sound of a lost or injured fawn may bring her in, whether she has offspring of her own or not. Fawn calls will work later in the season, too, but not as well, and there are several types of fawn calls.

The lost-fawn bawl is high pitched and fairly long and drawn out, simulating the plaintive cries of a fawn searching for its mother. This call will work any time of day but is most effective early and late in the day, when deer are most active and moving around (and thus, there is a higher probability of being heard). This is particularly true early in the season, when temperatures are high and deer don't move much during midday.

A fawn distress call is like the lost-fawn bleat but louder and much more excited. This is probably the one major exception in deer calling, in that the louder and more aggressive you are, the more effective it

■ Early in the season, a fawn bleat can be effective at luring in maternal does.

is. This call simulates a fawn in danger—caught in a fence or being attacked by a bobcat or coyote.

Like most calls, it doesn't always work. But when it does, the doe will often arrive quickly and on the run. The downside is that an approaching doe will be alert and on edge. This increases the chance she may "jump the string."

Whether bow or gun hunting, as soon as you see a deer approaching, stop calling.

When she gets closer, the doe will usually stop and begin searching for the source of the distress calls. She may only hold for an instant or two before bolting so take the first good shot you get.

You can make these calls with a variety of devices. Most of us probably remember as kids holding a blade of grass between our thumbs and blowing through it to make a squealing sound. Believe it or not, this will work on deer. The Algonquin Indians fashioned a similar bleat call from a folded leaf.

Today, most call manufacturers make mouth-blown fawn calls, and many predator and crow calls provide the same high-pitched, raspy sound. You can also get the necessary higher pitch by adjusting the reed on some grunt calls. One of the more recent designs, at least in the hunting market, is the can call. It is a handheld call that makes a bleat when you tip it upside down. Before they were marketed for hunting, I used to buy them at the local five-and-dime store, where they were sold as a novelty calf call. One season I even borrowed my daughter's stuffed cow doll, which had one sewn inside—and called several deer with it.

Doe Calls

Another good early-season doe call is the greeting grunt. This is simply a soft, one-note grunt, slightly higher pitched than a buck grunt. Like soft turkey clucks and

■ **Early in the season, when leaves are on the trees and visibility is poor, don't be afraid to call blindly, as unseen deer could be close by.** COURTESY OF MANUFACTURER

purrs, deer use it to alert one another to their presence. It is a relaxed call, and response is typically casual; deer are social animals and seek out others of their kind. Though more effective on does, it will occasionally work with bucks, too. And it can be used throughout the fall.

The greeting grunt can be used to call deer as well as merely to put them at ease. I once used it to lure a doe out of a dense patch of brush barely 40 yards away. She even grunted back as she calmly fed her way toward me. However, when she finally came within bow range, I missed, and she darted back into the underbrush. I grunted again, and out she came, allowing me a second shot. Unfortunately, the results were the same.

How and when to call will depend on circumstances. In the early fall, when leaves are still on the trees and visibility is poor, is a good time to call "blind." An unseen deer may be close by. The same holds true for hunting in thick cover or near bedding areas.

Your primary objective is to get the deer's attention and get them coming toward you. Once you've accomplished that, it's often best to cease calling. You want the deer to come to your location without pinpointing your exact position and possibly giving yourself away. If they hang up or turn away, they may need a little more coaxing, but don't overcall. In addition to giving yourself away, overcalling may also seem unnatural to deer, putting them on edge.

Buck Calls

Let's face it, while some of us (bowhunters, especially) may try to call the occasional doe, most of us are trying to call a buck. Fortunately, bucks seem to be susceptible to a wider range of calls, many of which also have some seasonality to them. In addition to knowing when to use which calls, you also need to know how much to call—and that can vary considerably based on circumstances.

Pre- and Postrut

For purposes of calling bucks, the deer season can be divided into two segments: the rut and the pre- and postrut periods. Early in the fall, when bucks are in bachelor groups, nonaggressive "attention" grunts can be used to stimulate the social curiosity of the bucks. These nonthreatening sounds prompt a more direct and less cautious response. You're trying to work on their curiosity more than their rut-driven instincts. You can also use minor doe calls like doe bleats. The same holds true for the postrut period, when you should back off from aggressive modes to softer contact sounds.

The Rut

Though bucks can be called in early in the season, you'll have your best results during the rut. Bucks are roaming all hours of the day. This, and their aggressive behavior, significantly increases the effectiveness of your calling. Now's the time for you, too, to get aggressive.

■ Bucks can be tough to call early and late in the season. But once the rut kicks in, that changes dramatically.

The simplest and most common rut call is the grunt. A buck grunt is deeper than a doe's and is most often made when he is seeking a doe. To another buck it represents both the possibility of a hot doe in the area and a potential rival.

Another, similar call is the tending grunt. It is the sound a buck makes when pursuing a hot doe and typically consists of several short, deep grunts given in quick

repetition. The number, duration, and cadence can vary considerably according to the intensity of the chase and the individual deer.

Bucks that are merely approaching a doe to see if she's ready to breed are often less vocal and may give a few longer grunts. They may also do this if they smell a hot doe but cannot see her. Conversely, I've heard bucks chasing a hot doe grunt almost with every breath, from the time they came into view until they went out of site. Here, the grunts are typically short and choppy. By imitating this call, you're conveying to other bucks in the vicinity that there is a doe in heat in the area. Thus, this is a great call to lure bucks out of thick cover, particularly dominant bucks who are anxious to see what upstart is tending "their" does.

■ When pursuing a hot doe, a buck will sometimes make a tending grunt, which consists of several short, deep grunts given in quick repetition.

Another good rut call is the breeding bawl. The effectiveness of this call has been more recognized recently with the popularization of so-called "can calls" (those little, tip-up canisters you used to be able to buy at the five-and-dime). When a doe is ready to breed but there are no suitors around, she'll announce her intentions with a drawn-out bleat or bawl, slightly deeper in tone than a fawn bawl. This call works best during the rut's chase phase but will work prior to and just after as well. It's also less threatening to subordinate bucks.

Conversely, the snort-wheeze is a highly aggressive call. When two mature bucks encounter one another during the rut, their first means of communication is body language. Ears back and hackles raised, they'll approach one another. The subordinate buck will usually back down and issue some subtle submissive gesture. Sometimes, however, a hot doe can make an ordinarily subordinate buck more aggressive. If he persists, the tending buck may snort-wheeze, as a warning that the rival suitor had better back off, or else. The snort-wheeze is similar to the sound a deer makes when it "snorts" or "blows," except that it is preceded by three short blows. To imitate it, whisper "dut, dut, dut, daaaaaah," as loudly and forcefully as you can into cupped hands—or use a call designed for that purpose.

When and How Much

A common question among hunters is how much to call when you're not seeing

■ After you've gotten a buck's attention, you need to take his temperature—look for a reaction. If he starts coming your way, it's time to stop calling.

deer. Calling about every fifteen minutes is probably a good rule of thumb, whether you're seeing deer or not. Remember, bucks can be roaming all day long, so don't get discouraged if your calling doesn't attract anything right away.

When deer are present, you may need to adopt a different strategy. The first step is to get the buck's attention, sort of like saying, "Hey, I'm over here." If the deer shows indifference, call again; he may not have heard you. If he did, you may need to reassure him with another grunt that says, "Yes, that is what you heard."

Then you need to take his temperature—look for a reaction. If the deer's interested at all, he'll turn and look your way. If he's not alarmed, he may adopt an aggressive posture, with ears back and the hair standing up on his back. This is a good sign. Or he may approach in a nervous posture, stiff-legged, wide-eyed, and with ears up—scanning for danger. This is particularly true of subordinate bucks that may be worried about getting the tar knocked out of them. Either way, if the deer starts coming your way, quit calling.

BE SUBTLE

As with turkey calling, the best advice is to err on the side of caution, at least until you gain more confidence and experience. The biggest mistake hunters make in both sports is overcalling. This may be especially true of deer hunters, as deer are considerably less vocal than turkeys. In general, calling should be soft and sparse (bear in mind there are exceptions to every rule). A deer's hearing is almost as keen as its sense of smell, and like a turkey, it can pinpoint your location by sound, sometimes long before they're within sight.

Understanding body language is key because you may need to adopt a different strategy if you get a negative reaction. If the deer acts as though he's uninterested or scared, you should back off the pressure. If he leaves unalarmed, you can always try another day, when he's in the right mood. But if you alarm the deer, you may never see him again from that stand.

Rattling

The basic concept of rattling is that by imitating the sound of sparring or fighting bucks, you pique the curiosity and aggressiveness of other bucks. Just as with humans, nothing gathers a crowd like a good fight. And like calling, rattling activity varies throughout the season. In the early fall increased testosterone increases aggression, prompting bucks to begin sorting out the dominance hierarchy or pecking order. Part of this is done through casual sparring that usually ends up being more of a shoving match than actual combat. I've watched young bucks sparring in early fall on several occasions, and at times the meshing of antlers seemed almost delicate.

Thus, early season rattling should be soft and sparse. This is best described as "tickling" antlers together.

Again, these are generalities, and there's an exception for every rule. I can recall one early October afternoon when, somewhat out of boredom, I picked up my antlers and imitated a long, loud bout.

Very early in the season, a doe decoy may be a better option. Deer are social animals, and at this time of year they seek out others of their kind. A relaxed, feeding, or bedded doe is more likely to attract other deer than an alert or aggressively postured one.

You can also use more than one decoy. In fact, during the peak of rut using a buck and a doe can sometimes tip the balance on skittish deer and send dominant bucks into fits. The only thing a buck hates more than a rival is a successful rival, and if he sees another buck with a doe, he's liable to come in with fire in his eyes.

Under almost any circumstances a decoy can be made even more effective by adding motion. Deer, especially does, don't always react positively to decoys. There may be several reasons, but I believe a big one is their immobility. How many times have you watched one deer suddenly come upon another one or a group? The heads go up, and there's a staring match that may last several minutes. Finally, one deer breaks the stalemate by flicking its tail. It's a very subtle body language signal that essentially says, "Everything here is okay."

Add that capability to your decoy and it could well mean the difference between success and failure. Some decoys actually have that function on a remote control. You can fashion one with a white rag and a piece of fishing line or simply add some toilet tissue and let the wind do the work.

Another way to enhance your decoy's effectiveness is with calls. First, they attract attention to your location and then to your decoy. Second, they add more realism. Which calls to use will vary with circumstances. During the peak of rut, tending grunts work well, particularly if you're using a buck-doe combo. Aggressive buck grunts and growls are also effective as they enhance the challenge aspect of the decoy.

Safety must always be your number-one consideration when using decoys. Consideration for other hunters should be number two. Some decoys are quite realistic and could attract unwanted attention from other hunters, particularly on heavily hunted areas. You may get away with it during the bow season, but it's best to leave the dekes home unless you're on private land where access is monitored and restricted. Forget about public land during firearms season.

Conclusion

Rattling, calling, and decoys won't make you a better hunter, but if you're already a good one, it can make you more successful. Perhaps the most important piece of advice to consider is not to get discouraged. More often than not these techniques won't work. But when they do results can be exciting. It's also important to remember that the above techniques are merely guidelines, not rules. Deer don't read the rule book, anyway. If you find something else that works, do it.

CHAPTER ELEVEN

Scents and Cover Scents

Ask an old veteran deer hunter what the recipe for successfully outwitting a wary whitetail is and he might tell you you've got to think like a deer, act like a deer, even sound like a deer. That's certainly true, but he'd have left out what could be the most important ingredient: smell like a deer.

Let's face it; a deer's sense of smell is the most important of its five senses (sometimes I think they have six) when it comes to both communicating and avoiding danger. Without seeing or hearing it, deer can tell when another animal—human, deer, or otherwise—is nearby or has been by recently. From another deer's scent, which may be hours or even days old, they can distinguish sex, social status, and breeding condition. So the key to overcoming a whitetail's strongest sense is first, trying not to smell like something they want to avoid (predator, human) and second, trying to smell like something they want to be near (food, other deer).

Deer use their sense of smell to avoid danger and as an important means of communication.
COURTESY OF MANUFACTURER

To be consistently successful, you've got to be odor free. This includes your body, clothing, and equipment. COURTESY OF MANUFACTURER

Odor Suppression

While using scents to attract deer could be considered an option, being scent free is mandatory, particularly for the bowhunter. Suppressing or masking human odor can be accomplished in several ways, including odor elimination, clothing, and treatments.

When it's warm or you're on the move, you sweat. Don't be afraid to carry some scent-suppressing spray with you and spray down your clothing, especially your hat, from time to time. COURTESY OF WILDLIFE RESEARCH CENTER

Applications

A variety of products exist that are designed to eliminate human (or other unnatural) odors. The most common and widely used are odor-reducing chemicals. They work in two ways: one, by reducing odors at the molecular level and two, by killing bacteria, which are the primary source of body odor. They come as nonaerosol sprays, solids, gels, or powders, which you apply to your body or clothing or both, and as soaps and detergents for washing both body and clothing.

Clothing

Another way to suppress your odor is by wearing clothing designed to do just that, and there are several types. The most common ones use odor-absorbing activated carbon fused to a fabric layer or membrane. Some use a chemical with an odor-absorbing molecular structure permanently embedded into the fabric. Still others utilize a deodorant built into the fibers of the garment. There are some who question the effectiveness of these garments in controlling odor, especially over time. The way I look at it, they can't hurt, and even if they do work, you still have to be mindful of the wind.

Cover Scents

Finally, you can cover human scent by masking or disguising it with a stronger, natural scent. Commercially available cover scents come both as blends with scent-elimination sprays or as independent cover scents. They're available in a variety of animal, vegetable, and even mineral odors. Vegetable scents are typically derived from extracts of aromatic vegetation, such as cedar, fir, pine, sage, or soft and hard mast fruits; for example, apples or acorns. Animal cover scents are usually urine from furbearers: fox, raccoon, skunk. The latter will mask human odor but should be used sparingly, as they may also arouse curiosity or suspicion (not to mention the ire of whoever does your laundry). Mineral scents or earth scents smell like dirt. In all cases the key is to pick an odor that is familiar to deer in the area you hunt.

Attractant Scents

The most popular and most widely used scents are attractant scents. They can be divided into three general categories: hunger or food scents, curiosity or appeasement scents, and attractant scents or sex attractants.

Food

Food scents attract deer by smelling like their favorite foods, such as apples, acorns, or persimmons. Again, the key is to pick a scent that is familiar in the area you hunt. Food scents are probably of limited utility. If the foods you're trying to imitate do occur in the area, the deer already know where they are and will go there instead. However, you just might be able to pique the curiosity of a passing deer enough to bring him into range.

Curiosity

Speaking of curiosity scents, pure curiosity scents work differently from food scents, representing a foreign yet still attractive odor. They typically consist of some type of strong food- or animal-based scent such as anise oil, musk, or vanilla. As far as I know, anise and vanilla do not occur naturally in the whitetail's range. Yet for some reason, deer sometimes seem inexorably attracted to them. In addition to pure scents, several manufacturers also market blends, which may contain a mixture of urine, food scents, and "secret" ingredients.

Attractants

The largest and most widely used group of scents includes those that smell like deer. These include urine- and glandular-based scents and often combinations of the two.

■ **"Salting" an active scrape with scent could heat it up. You can also make your own mock scrapes to try to entice a rutting buck into range.** COURTESY OF WILDLIFE RESEARCH CENTER

it will, in turn, do the same. If you're not finding rubs where you hunt, make some.

It's helpful if you can find some rubs in the vicinity. Bucks will often show a preference for certain types of trees, often the most aromatic, and your mock rubs will be more effective if you can find the same type of tree. They'll also be more effective if you place them in areas where deer ordinarily travel. All you need to do is scrape off some bark, exposing the cambium underneath with a knife, hatchet, or wood rasp. The rubs should be from about 18 inches to 3 feet off the ground. You might have more success if you also apply some scent to the rub.

Mock scrapes can be similarly used to lure deer where you want them. Again, the key is to place them where deer regularly travel and simulate natural conditions. The most important thing is to have an overhanging licking branch 4 to 5 feet above the scrape. In fact, sometimes that is stimulus enough to prompt deer into scraping on their own.

Once you find or make your overhanging branch, scrape away all the leaves and duff underneath, exposing bare soil. Scent control is vital here, so use rubber boots and rubber gloves. Sometimes this will be enough to attract deer, but your odds increase if you apply scent—buck or doe urine. That means keeping your scrape fresh, which requires frequent visits.

One way to avoid too much disturbance and human scent is to hang a scent dripper over the scrape. When warmed

■ **By creating mock scrapes and rubs, you can sometimes get deer to go where you want them to, rather than hunt them solely on their own terms.**

by the sun—therefore, during daylight hours—these devices drip scent slowly over a long period of time. This decreases the chances of disturbing the area and increases the chances of deer showing up while it's still light.

Conclusion

These are but a few of the many tactics you can employ to be more successful. Different situations call for different tactics, and you're limited only by the circumstances and your own imagination. Don't be afraid to experiment a little, even with something that seems radical. You may come up with something quite effective.

CHAPTER FOURTEEN

Planning a Trip

With whitetail populations soaring all across the continent, more and more hunters are looking beyond the borders of their own state or province for more or better hunting opportunities. Some hire guides, while others prefer the do-it-yourself approach. Regardless of which group you fall into, if you're thinking about an out-of-state hunt, there's a lot you can do to make it more enjoyable and, of course, more successful.

Choosing Your Destination

The first obvious step in the process is deciding where you want to hunt. You may already have a specific destination in mind—perhaps one of the whitetail

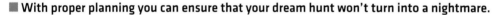

■ With proper planning you can ensure that your dream hunt won't turn into a nightmare.

meccas, such as Illinois, Kansas, or Saskatchewan. Or maybe you're looking for a trophy buck or high deer densities, and you want to know where the best odds lie. Either way you've got some homework to do in narrowing down your search.

Big bucks are turning up all over nowadays, but certain regions consistently produce a disproportionate number of them. Therefore, some areas offer significantly higher odds of bringing home venison. If you're a regular reader of outdoor magazines, you probably already have a pretty good idea of where those locations are. Another good resource for locating big-racked bucks is record books from one or more of the several trophy-recognition organizations—the Boone and Crockett Club, the Pope and Young Club, Safari Club International, and Buckmasters Trophy Records. Make sure you get the most recent books available, as they will show the latest trends, which do change over time. Sometimes an even better source, and one often overlooked by nonresidents, is state or regional trophy-club records. Some of these are operated by or through state fish and game agencies. If not, they can usually tell you how to contact them.

Booking a Hunt

Increasingly it seems that time is a key factor in how, when, and where we hunt. This is particularly true when hunting away from home. Hiring a guide is the most effective way to maximize limited hunting

---

HITTING THE HOT SPOTS

Your odds of bagging a really big buck are better where more of them exist, and research from the University of Georgia has shown three important variables influence which states consistently produce the most trophy bucks. First, there is an inverse relationship between the length of a state's regular firearms season and the number of record book entries. Second, states with firearms seasons after the rut had nearly ten times more Boone and Crockett entries than those with seasons before or during the peak of the rut. And third, states that allow shotguns only during their firearms season had nearly eight times more B&C entries than those allowing rifles. In all cases, reducing hunting pressure on bucks, particularly younger bucks, allows more of them to reach maturity and, thus, trophy age. Some of the better-known hot spots include Texas, Illinois, Kansas, Iowa, and Saskatchewan.

---

time because they do all the up-front work of scouting and stand placement. The only scouting you have to do is for an outfitter.

Choosing an Outfitter

If you decide to do a guided hunt, the next step is choosing an outfitter. Booking a guided hunt can be both an exciting and an anxious process. You've saved up your pennies, and you're finally going on that

■ **When interviewing a prospective outfitter, don't be afraid to ask for references, and then contact those references to get their impressions.**

"hunt of a lifetime." But there's a nagging doubt in the back of your mind. Even in the best of circumstances, things don't always work out as you had hoped, and hunting with an unscrupulous outfitter can turn a dream hunt into a real nightmare. There are, however, ways to reduce the risk of trusting your hunt to a stranger.

A good way to start is by thumbing through the back of your favorite hunting magazine or surfing the Internet, then requesting printed information. Once you've narrowed your search, you can start making phone calls and talking to

prospective outfitters. Attending an outdoor exposition offers the advantage of being able to talk to the outfitter, or his representative, face to face.

However you make contact, don't be misled by the outfitter—or by yourself. When you talk with him or her, make sure you ask the right questions, and listen carefully to the answers. Avoid what I call the optimism filter—hearing the good news and ignoring the bad.

Remember, the outfitter is trying to sell you a hunt, so he's going to present his product with a positive slant. When you ask about the quality of deer available, he'll probably first cite the top end. Make sure you ask for an average, and remember that it is just that. For instance, if the top end is 140 to 150 inches and the average is 125, that means a fair number of 100- to 110-inch bucks are being shot. Also, ask just how many of those top-end bucks are taken each year or, better yet, what percentage of hunters take them.

Success rate, expressed as some ratio of success relative to the number of hunters, is another figure outfitters use that could (unintentionally) mislead you. If an outfitter claims a 75 percent success rate, ask how he defines success. It could mean that 75 percent of all hunters killed a buck. Or it could mean that 75 percent of hunters killed a deer of either sex. Some outfitters will also define success as having a shot opportunity, whether you hit or miss. You should also ask what time period that pertains to. Was that just last season, or is it a long-term average?

You might also ask when during the season are most of the big bucks killed. Keep in mind, though, that if he's a good outfitter, those times often book up fast, sometimes a year or more in advance.

You also need to put these numbers into perspective, in terms of both geography and objective. In some states a success rate of 15 to 25 percent might be considered exceptional, while in others 50 percent might be more representative. Lower success rates could also be more common if the outfitter caters specifically to trophy hunters who are willing to pass up smaller bucks or to bowhunters.

Another thing you need to be absolutely clear on is exactly what you are getting for your money. There is no fixed definition of a guided hunt. Outfitters use various terms, such as fully guided, semiguided, or drop camp. A fully guided hunt usually means one guide per hunter. If you're hunting strictly from stands, a guided hunt may mean one guide dropping off and picking up several hunters. In any case, a guided hunt should include care of meat and trophy, which includes field dressing, caping, and preparing meat and trophy for transportation. Still, take nothing for granted.

Conversely, semiguided could mean one guide for several hunters or a guide who will show you some maps of the property, then send you on your way, which is fine if that's what you're looking for. Semiguided hunts may also not include care of your animal. You need to ask up front.

■ Make sure you find out in advance what services your guide offers. Terms like fully guided and semiguided can have different meanings from outfitter to outfitter.

One of the most important steps when booking a hunt is to ask for references— and use them. Most reputable outfitters will offer them anyway. Ask for the names of several hunters from different states, and ask for both successful and unsuccessful hunters. I've been on successful hunts that were just miserable and unsuccessful ones that were quite enjoyable.

Though it's sometimes difficult to gauge, one of the best indicators of a good outfitter is the amount of repeat business they get. If an outfitter offers that most of the best spots have already been booked by last year's hunters, you might want to get on his waiting list, book for the following year, or take a less desirable time in hopes of moving up the ladder.

There are also some things you can do to improve the quality of your hunt when you get there. One of the best pieces of advice is to never guide the guide. You may have plenty of deer hunting experience, but he has local knowledge, which is what you're paying for. Also, if you have any specific needs or constraints such as diet or physical limitations, be sure to make that known to your outfitter up front.

Booking Agencies

You can reduce a lot of both the guesswork and the real work involved with booking a hunt by using a booking agency. Start by observing some of the same rules. Look for someone who has been around, and ask for references.

They are professionals, and their primary responsibility is to spend their time and money evaluating outfitters so you don't have to. However, the hunt-package cost to the client should be the same whether he books through an agent or not.

Many agents will also handle other accommodations such as travel to and from the outfitter and any necessary layover lodging. The really good ones will provide you with an itinerary, a description of hunting conditions and accommodations, and a list of what you need to bring.

Do It Yourself

If you prefer to be in total control of your hunt or even if you merely want to save a few bucks, you can set up your own non-resident hunt. It just takes a little more planning and a little more time. And the more work you do ahead of time, the happier you'll be with the results.

Getting Started

Assuming you've selected a specific state or province, the next step is to contact that state's fish and wildlife agency. You can save considerable time if you have Internet access, as every state has a Web site loaded with pertinent information. You just need to know what to look for.

One very helpful bit of information is recent harvest statistics. If available, try to

■ **When researching your destination, look for places that offer a realistic opportunity at the class of deer you're looking for.**

get several seasons' worth of data. Weather conditions or other environmental factors could produce an aberrant season, but figures from multiple years will better illustrate long-term trends.

Again, you need to define your parameters to know what to look for. If you're after higher odds for success on any deer, look for where the highest deer densities are, which may be expressed as either the total number of deer killed or the number of deer killed per square mile. The latter is often a better indicator, as habitat, hunting conditions, pressure, and land area can vary considerably from unit to unit. High kill figures for a given unit may mean lots of deer, or it could mean a large unit. A little hint here: You may actually want to focus your attention on units adjacent to those with both high deer and high human densities. Deer densities will likely be similar, but hunting pressure may be considerably lower.

If, on the other hand, you're after big bucks, you may want to look for the frequency distribution of ages of adult bucks (1½ years or older), if available. Some states only record the percentage of yearling bucks in the harvest, which means the remainder could be anywhere from 2½ to 5½+ years of age. This is still useful, as a high percentage of yearling bucks is usually indicative of high hunting pressure and thus a good index of what's available—mostly yearling bucks. A better index is the number of mature bucks in the harvest. More mature bucks in higher age

LICENSES

Many states also allow you to purchase licenses online or download license applications, saving days or even weeks of waiting time. If you don't have online access, they still answer phone calls and letters. Regardless, once you've committed to a specific location, find out exactly what you need for licenses, permits, or tags, and get them as far in advance as possible. If at all possible, don't wait until you arrive to purchase your license. Arriving the night before opening day only to learn that the local license agent is closed or sold out of tags can put a real damper on your hunt—I know from experience.

classes mean greater trophy potential. In such cases, however, there's often a trade-off—fewer deer.

If you can't find this information on the Internet, don't be afraid to talk directly with a biologist. Remember, they work for you, the license-buying public, whether you're a resident or nonresident. Just bear in mind that they're busy folks and you don't want to waste their time. Tell them exactly what you're looking for, and have some specific questions ready.

The next step in planning your out-of-state hunt is to obtain topo maps and aerial photos, which we discussed in chapter 7. With these you can literally map out your hunt at home, saving valuable time when you finally arrive at your destination.

You'll more than likely be hunting on public land, so be sure to request information on public lands that are open to hunting in your area of interest. This can include federal, state, and local properties. Most state and federal agencies will have maps and brochures describing habitat and what game can be found, facilities, access points, and any special regulations or permits needed. Several states also have walk-in programs, where private lands are open to hunters through cooperative agreements.

One of the most useful items you can obtain for your trip is an atlas. DeLorme Mapping Company has an *Atlas and Gazetteer* for every state in the United States. In addition to detailed road maps and crude topography, these books also contain detailed lists of public lands, recreational areas and facilities, and, often, state agency contacts.

You're going to need a place to stay, such as a motel, cabin, or campground. You can get this information off the Internet or by contacting a local chamber of commerce. This is something you'll want to do early, as the best places will book up fast.

If you're planning a do-it-yourself hunt, you may want to think long term. In other words, it may take a season or two to

■ **Planning your own out-of-state hunt is a good way to save money and offers added satisfaction for the do-it-yourself types.** COURTESY OF MANUFACTURER

really get to know an area. If it's logistically possible, you could also make an advance scouting trip, which will add more value to your precious hunting time. If you do, don't be afraid to talk to local folks. They may be able to offer some advice and possibly even some leads on private land that you can gain access to.

CHAPTER FIFTEEN

Shot Placement and Recovery

Every hunter goes afield intending to recover the animal he shoots. Proper shot placement can go a long way toward that end. However, oftentimes considerable effort must be expended to locate a downed animal. Then, good tracking skills can help to reduce the time and effort necessary and increase the odds of a successful recovery.

Shot Placement

Once you pull the trigger or release the bowstring, there's no calling that projectile back. Therefore, you need to know with reasonable certainty that it's going to hit where you're aiming and that the hit will inflict a lethal wound. The solution to the first part involves enough practice to be proficient with your equipment and

■ A clean kill and a short tracking job are every hunter's goal. However, sometimes things go awry. When they do, take your time, be diligent and persistent, and your efforts should prevail.

■ Once you release the bowstring or pull the trigger, there's no calling that arrow or bullet back. You need to know with reasonable certainty that it's going to hit where you're aiming and that the hit will inflict a lethal wound.

making sure everything is in good working order. The second part requires knowledge of the deer's anatomy.

The object is to inflict a mortal wound. How best to do this can vary, to some degree, between bows and guns. In very general terms arrows kill by causing hemorrhaging, while bullets kill with shock and trauma. As a broadhead passes through an animal, it severs blood vessels, causing blood loss. If it remains in the animal, it will continue to cut, causing additional blood loss. A bullet passing through an animal has the same effect. But it also has considerably more energy. In addition

to simple blood loss, it also causes massive trauma and damage to soft tissue and bone. For these reasons the gun hunter has a bit more leeway in terms of shot placement.

The optimum shots for both gun and bow hunters are broadside or quartering-away chest shots. A broadside shot offers the largest target and room for error and will hit both lungs and possibly the heart. A slightly quartering-away shot offers a smaller target area. However, puncturing the diaphragm will compromise the pressure differential between the chest and abdomen, collapsing the lungs much faster.

THE WHITETAIL EXPOSED

Knowing what lies beneath can help immensely in shot placement. COURTESY NATIONAL BOWHUNTER EDUCATION FOUNDATION

The gun hunter has the additional option of shoulder or neck shots. When properly placed, they will drop a deer in its tracks. However, they must be precisely placed. This means you need a solid rest and complete confidence in your weapon. A few inches off the mark with a chest shot still means a dead deer. This may not be the case, however, for a shoulder or neck shot.

Two more or less reliable options for the gun hunter are straight on or straight away. The major drawback of the straight-on shot is that if you're an inch or two off your mark, your bullet will be hitting the heavy leg bones, shoulders, and ribs designed to protect the deer's most vulnerable area. The straight-away shot or Texas heart shot can be lethal but also very messy, as the bullet must first pass through the gut to reach the chest cavity.

Stand hunters must remember that the higher they go, the smaller their target area. Shots from a steep downward angle are more inclined to hit the spine or shoulder and may only hit one lung. On any steeply angled shot, whether taken from a stand or on the ground, it's a good idea to try to envision where the far side of the animal is and where the bullet or arrow

■ Don't shoot—this deer's vitals are obscured by a tree. Wait for him to step forward and offer a clean shot.

will exit. This will help you compensate for the angle.

If you are at all in doubt, don't shoot. Bad shots too often lead to long, anxious blood trails and lost animals. If you have a poor shot angle, or there is brush or some other obstacle in the way, wait for a better opportunity. It's better to wait or pass up the shot than to risk a bad shot.

Recovery

Good shot or bad, unless the animal drops within sight, you're going to have to go looking for it. If you've made a good shot, that task shouldn't be too difficult, though sometimes it is. If you've made a bad shot, you've got your work cut out for you. In any case, the job begins the moment you shoot.

■ A quartering-away shot is ideal, but remember to concentrate on the far shoulder and compensate for the angle or your shot might be too far forward.

Postimpact

When possible, try to determine where the animal was hit. Sometimes you can do this with behavioral clues. For example, a heart-shot deer will often buck, jumping straight up in the air or kicking its hind legs up high before bolting. A deer shot in the low shoulder or leg may run erratically. A paunched deer will often hunch up and walk or trot away in a humped-up posture. Lung-shot deer can react in a variety of ways, from bolting on impact to showing complete indifference, so an ambiguous reaction is not necessarily a bad thing.

The next thing to do is note where the animal was standing when hit and in which direction it went after the hit. Also try to note where you last saw or heard it. It's helpful if you look for a particular feature, like a tree or other landmark the deer passed by. Try to take a compass reading on the deer's direction of travel. It's important that you do all this right away, especially if you're in an elevated stand. You're excited, and after you get down, things look different.

How long you wait before taking up the trail may well be the deciding factor in whether, or how easily, you will recover your deer. It is always better to err on the conservative side. If the animal is down, it's not going anywhere. If it's not, you risk losing it.

Bowhunters should wait a minimum of half an hour before they even climb down from their stand. In general, gun shots can

---

FINDING BLOOD

Under poor lighting conditions blood can be difficult to see. There are several commercial products available that are designed to make it more visible. A very handy substitute that you may have around the house is hydrogen peroxide. When it comes in contact with blood, it fizzes. Carry some in a spray container, and spray the ground if you lose the blood trail.

---

be followed up sooner. In either case, this waiting period is not only for better odds of recovery but also for safety. It forces you to calm down and gather your thoughts.

It also gives you a chance to visualize the shot in your mind. As you replay the action in your mind's eye, concentrate on where and how the deer was hit. Was it forward or back? Which way was the deer facing: broadside, quartering to, or away? All these things may help you determine when it's time to take up the trail.

The next step, before you actually take up the trail, is to look for physical evidence that might help determine where the deer was hit. A good mantra for the bowhunter is to go to the arrow—the arrow tells all. A blood-stained arrow is generally good news, and the brighter red the blood the better. Remember the phrase: *A for away*. The heart pumps oxygenated blood through the arteries, away from the heart/lung area, so it is bright red. Venous blood is flowing to the heart and is darker

■ **Brighter is better. Bright red blood usually indicates an arterial hit, which means the deer is more likely to bleed out.**

red, as it is oxygen depleted. Dark red blood could mean a muscular hit, which is not necessarily bad, if there is an ample amount.

A brown-stained arrow is bad news, but not hopeless. If you don't see blood but the arrow is wet or moist, smell it. If the deer was paunched, you should be able to detect the odor of stomach contents. A paunch shot is fatal, and you should find your deer, though it will take extra attention to details. For a paunch shot, wait a minimum of four to six hours before taking up the track.

As you look at the evidence, remember to be honest, and don't second-guess yourself. Being patient at this point also forces you to slow down so you don't overlook details. There are very few circumstances, except perhaps a faint blood trail and torrential rains, that require quick action at

TRACKING DOGS

Where legal, tracking dogs can be an invaluable asset to recovering deer. With a sense of smell that rivals a deer's, dogs are much better equipped to follow a trail than humans are. However, you would be ill-advised to use just any dog. Dogs that are not trained to follow wounded deer can become easily confused with all the smells of the forest and may end up following a perfectly healthy deer or some other critter.

Most states where tracking dogs are legal have a contact list.

■ **Where legal, tracking dogs can be a tremendous asset to recovering wounded deer.**

These folks are dedicated individuals and are usually quite eager to help out. For them the pleasure is seeing their dogs work out a trail and ensuring a happy ending.

■ **Predators and scavengers are a legitimate concern when deciding whether to leave an animal in the woods overnight. Ultimately you must weigh the odds and decide what course of action you think is best.**
COURTESY OF MANUFACTURER

this point. Even impending darkness is not cause to rush.

You should also be looking for other evidence of a hit, especially if you're hunting with a gun or your arrow didn't get complete penetration. If you find where the deer was standing, you should find dig marks in ground where it took off. You may be able to follow these marks for some distance in the absence of blood. I've dry-tracked deer for several hundred yards merely by getting down on my hands and knees and placing my fingers in the indentations made by the deer's hooves.

On the Track

A blood trail is like a good mystery. The more clues you gather, the easier it is to solve.

Most hunters' inclination is to follow just blood, but you should also be paying attention to tracks and other sign. Try to line out the tracks so you can predict where the deer will go should you run out of blood. Don't be afraid to get down to a deer's-eye view, either. At this level you can see what the deer was seeing. Unless it's on a dead, panic run, it will often take

INTERPRETING BLOOD

Blood can show certain characteristics that may indicate the type and severity of the wound.

■ Bright red blood often indicates a muscle or artery hit. Superficial flesh wounds and wounds to the extremities may bleed profusely at first but will often cease quickly. Arterial wounds will bleed profusely. Muscle wounds can be highly variable.

■ Bright red, frothy blood with lots of tiny bubbles usually means a lung hit; fewer, larger bubbles could be a neck or throat hit.

■ Dark red blood could indicate a liver or kidney hit.

■ Blood with greenish plant material and a foul odor means paunch.

■ Sprayed or spattered blood could indicate that either the animal was running or you hit a major artery.

■ Blood on both sides of the trail indicates a pass-through shot.

the path of least resistance—a trail or an opening in otherwise dense cover.

It's always a good idea to enlist help when you can. Another person means another set of eyes and a more objective second opinion. When tracking with more than one person, remember to be very quiet. Talk only in whispers, or use hand signals or whistles. You should also be listening very carefully, as you may hear the deer run off ahead of you. If that happens, it's best to back off and wait a while.

It's also especially important that you don't let anyone go ahead of the lead tracker. If it comes down to dry tracking, you may be looking for signs as subtle as bent-over grass or broken twigs, scuffed moss, and the like. Every animal that travels through the woods leaves some sign, and a wounded one usually leaves more and different sign. Learn to recognize it.

Tracks left by a wounded deer also provide clues. A wounded deer, especially one with a broken or injured leg, will show erratic tracks and drag marks. This can be especially helpful in identifying your deer's tracks if it gets into a tracked-up area. In snow, if there are multiple tracks, look for fresh soil thrown out by a running deer or places where snow has recently been knocked off limbs. If running tracks quickly change to walking tracks, it could mean the deer is close, or it could mean a paunch shot. You need to be on red alert. The same is true if the

■ **Blood on the snow is one of the easiest trails to follow. That's all the more reason to take your time and do the job right.**

track begins meandering, which could mean the deer is becoming disoriented due to blood loss.

Some hunters mark the trail with surveyor's tape. Unless you plan on removing it all when you're finished, toilet paper is a better choice. It will show up nearly as well but is biodegradable. As long as you can follow a visible blood trail, you may only need to mark it at lengthy intervals. If sign starts petering out, mark the point of last blood before moving on. If you have help, you may also want to leave someone at that point until you find more sign.

When All Else Fails

Don't use lack of blood as an excuse to give up. A wound may stop bleeding for any number of reasons. It could be plugged up with fat or tallow, and a high hit with no exit may bleed very little.

If you run out of sign entirely, it's time to begin a random search. Most hunters do circles around the point of last blood or sign, which is an effective method. Sometimes a better alternative is a grid search. Get as many people as you can, and line up closely enough so you can see the feet of the person next to you. Have one person be the leader, and work the line in a compass direction—go north to south or east to west.

If you have a general direction of travel, you should begin searching in that direction. It's unlikely, though certainly not impossible, that the animal will reverse direction, so concentrate your effort along and to either side of the general direction of travel. Take the grid line out to a landmark or obstacle where you don't think the deer will go. Then swing the line around. The outside man becomes the inside man, and you search back in the direction you came from. Ultimately, you will end up searching the entire area in a checkerboard pattern.

A few other generalities might help steer you in the right direction. Wounded

---

TRACKING LIGHT

If you hunt in the afternoon, you'll likely be following a blood trail after dark, which is why you should always carry a flashlight with you. A simple, handheld Maglite or headlamp will pick up a good blood trail, but you may need something stronger if the blood trail is troublesome. A four-cell flashlight or even a spotlight can dramatically increase visibility.

Still, I don't know exactly why, but nothing illuminates a blood trail better on a dark night than a Coleman lantern. The glass globe and delicate mantles make them difficult to keep in the truck, but I always have one on hand at home should I encounter a particularly difficult trail. However, the lantern provides 360 degrees of lighting. To keep the beam facing forward and eliminate glare from backlighting, I shield one side with aluminum foil.

deer are more inclined to go downhill rather than up. If they still have their wits about them, they will often head to very dense security cover, and if they're hit in the paunch, they'll go to water.

When you do find your deer, make sure it has expired before you try to handle it. There are many deer-hunting legends, some based on truth, of "dead" deer coming back to life and running off or injuring a hunter. Always approach from the rear, and touch the eye with a stick, arrow shaft, or gun barrel.

When to Give Up

Determining when to give up can (and should) be a gut-wrenching decision. You took the shot, and you owe it to the deer to exhaust all possibilities and resources to find it. If the grid search fails, go back the next day and look for crows, vultures, or coyotes. I once found a deer in North Carolina by letting circling vultures lead me to it.

If all your efforts ultimately fail, there's still something to be gained from your experience. Go over everything again. Ask yourself, "What went wrong? How could I have done things differently?" You can also take some solace in the fact that deer have an amazing vitality for life. If you honestly exhausted all avenues at your disposal to find the deer and came up empty, there's a very good chance the animal will survive.

FINDING YOUR WAY OUT

Keeping a cool head when blood trailing is important not only in finding your deer but also in finding your way back out. Too often hunters start on what they think will be a short blood trail only to find themselves far from where they started and "turned around."

If you have a GPS, you should have already marked your vehicle, camp, or house. Leave it on as you track, and if you have to go back for help, mark where you left off. Once you find your deer, your GPS may be able to show you a shorter way out than the way you came in.

CHAPTER SIXTEEN

From Field to Fire

You did it. The planning and preparation, the careful attention to detail in picking out the right equipment, the scouting, and the shooting practice all paid off. The object of all your efforts now lies lifeless at your feet, symbolizing a logical and successful conclusion to your hunt. But in a broader sense, it isn't over yet. There's still much that needs to happen between the field and the freezer or the trophy room to ensure a favorable conclusion to all your efforts. And the process begins almost immediately.

Field Dressing

Once you've officially "taken possession" of your prize, your first decision will be whether or not to field dress your deer on the spot. Traveling around the country, I've found that local customs vary. Southerners, especially, tend to take their deer out of the woods whole, while northerners most often dress theirs on the spot. Regardless, unless you're going to bone it out right away, you need to get your deer opened up and remove the entrails as soon as possible. Every moment that passes between the time the deer is killed and when it is eviscerated (gutted) increases the risk of tainting or spoiling the meat. And the warmer the temperature, the more critical it is to "empty out" your deer.

To begin the field-dressing process, lay the deer on its back. This is best done on

■ **The process of ensuring your game will provide fine table fare and a handsome mount begins as soon as you tie on your tag.**

■ I don't quite understand why anyone would want to drag an extra 20 or 30 pounds of useless weight through the woods unnecessarily, but customs vary around the country, and some hunters prefer to gut their deer back at camp rather than in the field.

level ground, but if the ground is sloped, face the deer's head uphill. It's also helpful if you can have someone hold the rear legs apart. Then follow these steps:

1. Cut only the skin around the anus or vent, being careful not to cut into the intestine itself. Try to make your cut deep enough into the pelvic canal to cut away any tissue connecting the vent to the canal.

2. Cut only the skin around the genitals (buck) or udder (doe), cutting back toward the vent as you pull them away from the body.

3. Tie a piece of cord or string around the rectum, cinch it tightly and knot it. You can now cut away the genitals or udder, above the knot, and discard them. The knotted cord will ensure that no urine or feces enter the body cavity when you pull the vent back through the body cavity.

4. At the base of the brisket (breastbone), make a shallow incision through the skin and belly muscle, being careful not to cut into the paunch (guts). You can do this by lifting the skin and muscle up and away from the body while simultaneously inserting the knife—blade up. Beginning at the base of the brisket, cut down the middle of the belly to the vent. It is critical that you avoid puncturing the paunch. Stomach contents can taint the meat, make a nasty mess, and introduce you to an aroma you will never forget. I've seen grown men lose their lunch with one whiff of paunch. This is best accomplished by first positioning your knife with the blade facing upward, then inserting two fingers (one on each side of the knife blade in the shape of a "V") in the slit. Use your two guide fingers to push the skin and muscle upward as you cut. Another way is to use a knife with a skinning blade.

5. If you don't intend to mount the deer, you can continue your cut up through the rib cage with a knife or saw, opening the

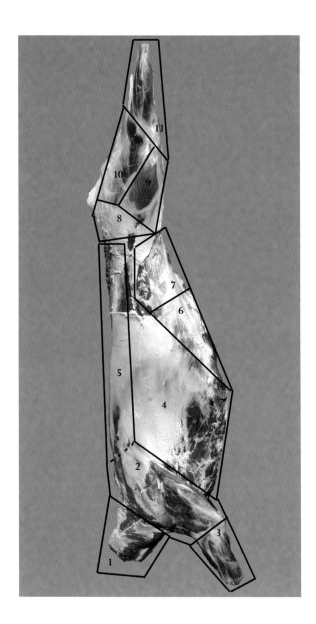

you ultimately prepare it for the table is limited by your own imagination and inspiration. When you finally sit down to eat, you will enjoy not only some of the finest organic protein on the planet, but you will also enjoy a particular sense of accomplishment in knowing it came about by your own hand.

HANG TIME

Hunters often hang their deer to "age" the meat, allowing natural enzymes to tenderize it.

The optimum temperature for aging is 32 to 38 degrees F. At this temperature range it can hang for as long as 10 days. Temperatures above 40 degrees F not only age meat faster but also may lead to spoilage. Therefore, aging above 40 degrees F is not recommended.

10. **Top round**—steak, roast

11. **Lower hind leg**—burger or stew

The purpose of this book is to help you get your venison from the woods to the freezer. The rest, as they say, is up to you. To borrow and corrupt an old proverb: Give a man a deer, and you feed him for a month. Teach a man to hunt, and you feed him for a lifetime. There are countless good cookbooks out there, many just for venison, filled with great recipes. How

CHAPTER SEVENTEEN

Scoring Your Antlers

Antlers are nature's art and that which stirs the soul of every deer hunter. And while some hunters are content merely to admire them for their inherent beauty, many feel a need to quantify them, so they can be measured against some relative scale. Several systems exist to do this.

The most commonly used and widely accepted method for measuring deer antlers was originated in 1949 by Grancel Fitz

■ Antlers are far more than mere bony appendages. They are the glorious artwork of nature that stirs the soul and captivates the mind of every hunter.

■ Antlers attach to the skull at a permanent point of attachment called a "pedicel." Just above this, the knobby, flared ring at the base of each antler is called a "burr." The rough textures, usually at the base of the main beam, just above the burr, are called "perlations."

for the Boone and Crockett Club's *Official Record Book of North American Big Game.* To this day, it is still considered the most equitable and is now recognized and used internationally as the standard method. Basically, it involves a combined measure of antler length, mass, and symmetry. The final score is a net score, calculated by deducting differences in symmetry between each side of the rack. By following the directions below, anyone can measure antlers with reasonable accuracy.

First, you'll need to know a little vocabulary. The basic whitetail antler is composed of several parts. The point of attachment, which is a permanent protrusion of the skull, is called a *pedicel.* Antlers (as opposed to horns) are deciduous; each year a new antler grows from this root. Just above the pedicel, at the base of each antler is a knobby, flared ring called a *burr.* The rough textures, usually at the base of the main beam just above the burr, are called *perlations.*

Racks are categorized as either *typical* or *nontypical.* A typical set of antlers consists of two main beams with several individual *points* or *tines* rising up, roughly perpendicular to the main beam. A typical rack is symmetrical, with evenly matched

■ **Even within typical racks there is considerable variation in shape and form.**

tines on both antlers. The first tines on each beam are most often called the *brow tines*, or *brow points*, though they have been attributed a variety of sometimes colorful names, such as "eye guards" and "'tater diggers." Traditionally, antler scorers called this point a *bez* (pronounced "bay"), but this term has largely gone out of use except with caribou and has been replaced with the less colorful term *G-1*.

The next tine, formerly called the *tres* (pronounced "tray"), is now simply *G-2*. Successive points are named and numbered in a similarly mundane fashion. Some purists believe that the true typical rack sports eight points and those bearing any more should be considered nontypical. Officially, as long as the tines are symmetrical, the rack is considered typical. Any asymmetrical antler growth is considered abnormal.

In our society relative value is often assessed on the basis of rarity. Thus, it is not surprising that the rarest and often most prized antlers are *nontypicals*. A nontypical rack can vary from the basic form described above in almost any and every way imaginable. And the reasons for these variations are as diverse, and sometimes as bizarre, as the racks themselves. Some of the more common nontypical manifestations of nontypical antler growth are drop, forked, or webbed tines; sticker, cheater, beauty, or kicker points; and cactus racks.

Interestingly, many of these seemingly unique variations are genetically based. Thus, you may find several bucks in a particular area that all have similar drop or forked tines or palmated beams. Though the reasons are not well understood, nontypical growth also sometimes results from injury to a limb. Even more surprising is

Barnes & Noble Booksellers #2658
11500 Financial Ctr Pkwy
Little Rock, AR 72211
501-954-7646

2658 REG:001 TRN:8238 CSHR:Will N

Tactics: Whitetail Hunting: Expert S
81599217895   T1
    @ 19.95)   19.95

otal   19.95
s Tax T1 (7.500%)   1.50
L   21.45
DEBIT   21.45
rd#: XXXXXXXXXXXXX0737

MBER WOULD HAVE SAVED   2.00

Thanks for shopping at
Barnes & Noble

27A   11/05/2011 10:19AM

CUSTOMER COPY

through Barnes & Noble.com via PayPal. Opened music/DVDs/audio may not be returned, but can be exchanged only for the same title if defective.

<u>After 14 days or without a sales receipt</u>, returns or exchanges will not be permitted.

Magazines, newspapers, and used books are not returnable. *Product not carried by Barnes & Noble or Barnes & Noble.com will not be accepted for return.*

Policy on receipt may appear in two sections.

Return Policy

<u>With a sales receipt</u>, a full refund in the original form of payment will be issued from any Barnes & Noble store for returns of new and unread books (except textbooks) and unopened music/DVDs/audio made within (i) 14 days of purchase from a Barnes & Noble retail store (except for purchases made by check less than 7 days prior to the date of return) or (ii) 14 days of delivery date for Barnes & Noble.com purchases (except for purchases made via PayPal). A store credit for the purchase price will be issued for (i) purchases made by check less than 7 days prior to the date of return, (ii) when a gift receipt is presented within 60 days of purchase, (iii) textbooks returned with a receipt within 14 days of purchase, or (iv) original purchase was made through Barnes & Noble.com via PayPal. Opened music/DVDs/audio may not be returned, but can be exchanged only for the same title if defective.

<u>After 14 days or without a sales receipt</u>, returns or exchanges will not be permitted.

Magazines, newspapers, and used books are not returnable. *Product not carried by Barnes & Noble or Barnes & Noble.com will not be accepted for return.*

Policy on receipt may appear in two sections.

that the antler deformation usually occurs on the opposite side from the injury. Most amazing of all is that antler has memory; once an antler has taken on an aberrant form or characteristic, that characteristic will often return in subsequent antlers, even after the injury has healed!

Scoring a Typical Rack

The following are cookbook instructions to measure a typical rack. Nontypical racks can be problematic and will be discussed afterward.

To score a rack you'll need a few items. Obviously, you need a measuring device. Official scorers use a ¼-inch flexible steel tape. Any suitable substitute will suffice for a preliminary scoring; for instance, a flexible plastic or cloth sewing tape (though they tend to stretch and are less accurate). Another handy device often used by official scorers is a length of brake cable from a bicycle. Last but not least, you'll need a pencil and a score sheet. You can set up a blank page like the accompanying score

the sheet. Note
: taken to the
of a measure-
hths, round to
asure falls pre-
up.

urements are
:o the official
sed reference
lumns, record

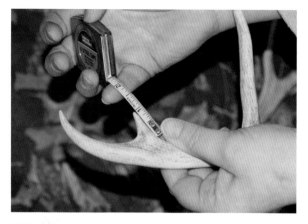

■ **To be counted, a point must project at least 1 inch from the nearest edge of the main beam, and its length must exceed the width of its base.**

A. Number of Points on Each Antler — This system uses what is sometimes referred to as "eastern count." It is a count of the number of projections or tines on each antler or beam, including the brow tines and the terminal point of the main beam. To be counted, a point must project at least 1 inch from the nearest edge of the main beam, and its length must exceed the width of its base. Again, the tips of the main beam are also counted as points. "Western count" refers to the points on one antler and does not count brow tines.

B. Tip-to-Tip Spread — This is one of three measures of space other than antler (and these measures are not used by some scoring systems; for instance, Buckmasters Trophy Records). Simply measure the distance between the tips of the main beams. To be accurate, this measurement should be taken perpendicular to the long axis of the skull. If a straight line from tip to tip is not perpendicular, you must project an imaginary line.

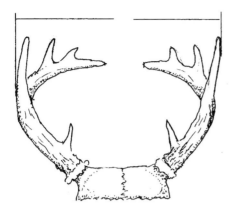

 Greatest outside spread is a measure of the greatest distance between the outermost projection on either antler. In most cases it will be measured from the outside of the main beams, unless there are points that project beyond the beams.

C. Greatest Spread—Also called outside spread, this is a measure of the greatest distance between the outermost projection on either antler and is also taken between perpendiculars at right angles to the centerline of the skull (in other words, parallel to the top of the skull). In most cases it will be measured from the outside of the main beams, unless there are points that project beyond the beams.

D. Inside Spread—The greatest inside spread is measured at the widest point on the inside of the main beams. This number is entered in Column 1 of the score sheet. If this measurement exceeds the length of the longest antler beam, the latter measurement is used instead, and the difference is entered in Column 4.

E. Total Lengths of Abnormal Points—Typical racks may still contain some points that are not consistent with the symmetry and shape of the rack—sometimes referred

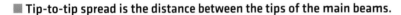 Tip-to-tip spread is the distance between the tips of the main beams.

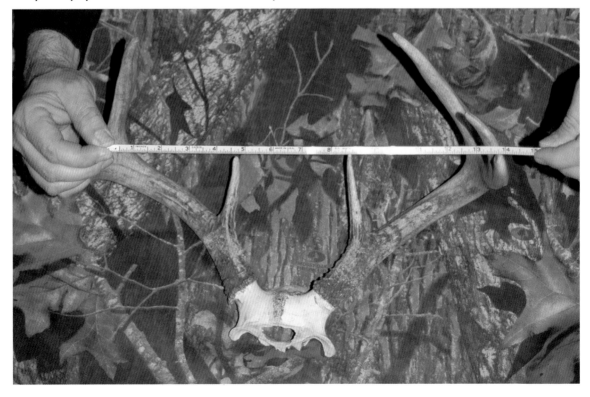

CHAPTER EIGHTEEN

Introducing Youngsters to Hunting

With whitetail populations booming and quality management gaining momentum across North America, the future of deer hunting looks very bright indeed. However, that future depends on recruiting youngsters into the sport. Otherwise, we could one day find ourselves with plenty of deer to hunt and no one to hunt them. Then, rather than the magnificent animals we know them to be,

■ Teaching a youngster to hunt is an important and rewarding experience that will ensure the future of hunting.

deer would be little more than a nuisance, a pest to be disposed of by hired guns. For that reason, it behooves all of us to introduce youths to deer hunting.

And that is no small challenge. Youngsters are bombarded with instant-gratification activities, such as television or computer and video games. Increasingly, those brought up in urban areas or broken homes have fewer opportunities to spend time out of doors. As parents or mentors we need to create more opportunities. We also need to ensure that they have a safe, enjoyable, and positive learning experience. Otherwise we'll lose them to the other temptations. What follows is some advice and instruction on just how to go about that sometimes daunting but immensely rewarding task.

Safety Courses

Perhaps the most important single act you can do to ensure that your young hunter has a safe and enjoyable experience is to enroll him or her in a hunter-safety course. Many of you could probably do a stand-up job yourselves, but children often learn better in a structured environment. The curriculum is designed so that they are given instruction in all of the important facets of hunting, including firearms safety, use, and handling; wildlife identification; survival and first aid; and ethics and responsibility. If you want to be more involved in their education, take the course with them. It might be more reassuring to them

and can strengthen the bond between you. Most states now require them of first-time hunters anyway.

Courses are typically run by volunteer instructors, who donate their time and energy for the cause. Some may charge a small fee, but most are free. The money for course materials and other expenses comes from the Federal Aid in Sport Fish and Wildlife Restoration Program (also known as the Pittman-Robertson Act), which is funded from taxes on sporting arms and ammunition. Each state receives a portion, which must be used for programs that benefit wildlife habitat and management programs, including hunting education.

For more information on hunter education, you can contact your state fish and game agency or check out the International Hunter Education Association's Web site at http://ihea.com.

Stages of a Hunter

In their course curriculum the International Hunter Education Association (IHEA) lists the five stages of a hunter. It's important for us as teachers and mentors to understand that new hunters must go through a learning process, an evolution of sorts, as they develop their skills. While not everyone will go through each stage, or in order, they still provide a fairly accurate guideline to hunter evolution.

The first stage is the shooter stage. A firearm can be a very intriguing tool to youngsters, who want to be able to use it as quickly as possible. In general kids think of good hunting as lots of shooting. Patience and restraint are difficult concepts for younger hunters, who have short attention spans.

The best remedy for this is to let them do lots of shooting, before they hunt. Take them out to the range, and let them shoot until they're sick of it. This is also a good way to get them familiar and proficient with their firearm or bow.

The second stage is the limiting-out stage. Their primary goal is meeting their bag limit, and hunting becomes a numbers game. This is actually a common level for adult hunters as well. Many of us merely want to shoot a deer, any deer. After all, that's why we're out there. And depending on circumstances, this is probably a good level for young hunters to aspire to, as opposed to the next stage.

Third is the trophy stage. At this level the hunter becomes more selective about the individual animal to be shot. It's important to teach youngsters about such concepts as responsible stewardship and quality deer management, but those lessons will come a lot easier after they have achieved a certain level of success. Don't make them hold out for a trophy buck for their first deer. In time, if they become proficient, they may choose to do so themselves.

The fourth stage is the method stage. After the young hunter has experienced some success and gained some experience and confidence, it may be time to

■ It's important for us as teachers and mentors to understand that young hunters must go through a learning process, at their own pace, as they develop their skills.

try a different, more challenging method. Instead of a rifle, a muzzleloader or a bow may provide added challenge. Encourage this, but don't force it too soon. And if the youngster becomes frustrated, encourage persistence.

The final stage is the sportsman stage. Success is derived from the entire hunting experience: the challenge, being out of doors, and sharing time with other sportsmen and -women.

Introducing Youngsters to Firearms

As the above section illustrates, an important first stage for young hunters is shooting. Simply plinking in the backyard can be great fun and is sometimes enough to pique the interest of a potential hunter. It's also important because it provides a first opportunity to teach safe handling.

One of the easiest and least expensive ways to get started is with a BB or pellet gun. A safe air gun range is easy to set up in a backyard or basement. However, these guns must be handled according to the

■ **Proper safety and handling are key elements to ensuring your youngster will have a safe and enjoyable hunt.**

same safety rules as for firearms. Parents should stress that these are not toys, and youngsters should not use them without parental supervision, until they're ready.

The National Rifle Association (NRA) recommends users learn and instructors stress the following safety rules for air guns:

■ Always keep the gun pointed in a safe direction.
■ Always keep your finger off the trigger until ready to shoot.
■ Always keep the gun unloaded until ready to use.
■ Be sure of your target and what is beyond.
■ Eye protection must be worn by shooters and spectators.

Opportunities for Young Hunters

Seeing the declining number of young hunters, more and more states are implementing special seasons directed specifically at youths. They're typically a day or a weekend before the regular seasons open, which gives youngsters the first shot and potentially better odds of success.

Most states also offer youth hunting licenses for little or no cost as a way to encourage more participation. Even if there is a cost, it's minimal when compared to the price of a trip to the movies or an X-Box.

For a youngster's first hunt, there are a few things to bear in mind. Most

■ **Many states now offer special permits and seasons as a way to encourage young hunters.**

important, it should be fun. Don't stay out too long, especially if it's cold or the action is slow. Kids have a much shorter attention span than *most* adults.

Also, don't ever make them feel pressured. Remind them that it's about being outdoors and enjoying nature, and if they are successful, that's just icing on the cake. If they miss a shot, pour on the reassurance. Let them know that it happens to everyone. I'm sure most of us have a litany of tales we could tell about missed or botched opportunities.

And if they're not interested, don't force them. They may simply not be mature enough or may have other interests. In time they may develop an interest.

Or they may start out enthusiastically but lose interest over time. Even if they spend only a day or two afield with you, it could leave a lasting impression that will stay with them for the rest of their lives, and you want it to be a positive one.

Teach Your Children Well

As you take your young hunter out for the first time, don't miss out on a golden opportunity. As the previous chapters have pointed out, deer hunting is a lot more than sitting in the woods waiting to shoot something. Point out sign, such as tracks, rubs, and scrapes, and explain what they signify. Teach how to identify what foods

 Plenty of practice enables your youngster to become familiar and proficient with a gun or bow before hunting.

deer like to eat, where they may travel, and where they hide.

Teaching a youngster to hunt is an important rite of passage, a first step toward adulthood. In deer hunting, as in life, all we can do is to try to teach them right from wrong. Ultimately, they will choose their own path. But if we have done our job well, their journey will be successful.

■ As you take your young hunter out the first time, remember it should be a fun learning experience. Take time to point out sign, and teach the ways of the whitetail. COURTESY OF MANUFACTURER

About the Author

Bob Humphrey is a registered Maine guide, certified wildlife biologist, and an award-winning outdoor writer/photographer who has pursued America's most beloved big game animal for more than three decades. He has also developed a knack and a reputation for sharing his insight and experience through print, Internet and television media, and has published hundreds of articles in dozens of national magazines including: *Outdoor Life*, *Sports Afield*, *Buckmasters*, *North American Hunter*, and *Petersen's Bowhunting*.